S0-ASP-045

Out of the DARKNESS

JOY STINSON

MINDSTIR MEDIA

Out of the Darkness
Copyright © 2013 Joy Stinson. All rights reserved.

Published by Mindstir Media
1931 Woodbury Ave. #182 | Portsmouth, New Hampshire 03801 | USA
1.800.767.0531 | www.mindstirmedia.com

Printed in the United States of America
ISBN-13: 978-0-9894748-1-8
Library of Congress Control Number: 2013942920

In memory of Charlie Williamson

Chapter 1

CERTAIN MEMORIES SHOULD HAUNT US FOR SOME TIME; memories, though, should not taunt us, tease us, and torment us. My story—my memory—did all of that; yet, I survived. The excitement and anticipation of what was to come bore into me with a ferocity which I had never experienced previously. This night, our girls' night out, was, in my mind, an opposing view of the mundane life I had known of south Louisiana. What I anticipated, what I felt, somewhat resembled the nights of childhood sleepovers with friends; though, I could not fathom why anyone would include "sleep" in the word as that was always the farthest thought from our minds. And, while this night reminded me of one of those sleepovers, it was, in fact, the life before this night which was my sleep. For the past several years, I had been locked away in a dream under a shadow of darkness, drifting aimlessly, from raising my three young daughters while my husband worked out of town for a week, sometimes longer, to juggling other responsibilities in my life, and all the while, attempting at some level to keep the girl I was somewhere in the body of the woman I had become. Once, as a child, I was filled with energy and vitality; recently, however, when I looked at myself, I saw not who I was, but instead, I saw who I was becoming. My neurologist said my Young Onset Parkinson's Disease was progressing at a fast rate, and all I could see and think of was the bleak reality of wheelchairs, feeding tubes, and diapers. This ole gal—the spirit of my formative years—refused to accept defeat; I refused to let my body define me. This night was to be a new beginning for me—a new world in which I would awaken and discover the Joy I wanted to be. Tonight, with the darkness surrounding us, I would step into the light of becoming me.

Yet, as I sauntered into this new world of fun and excitement, I knelt and prayed. It was a prayer. It was not a prayer. It began—and ended—as my prayers to God did of late, with clinical, stifled words.

"Ok, it's me again, God. Help me get through another day, blah, blah, blah. Shouldn't I get some credit for that, God? I go to church every Sunday, plus I'm good at lip synching. Doesn't that count? And God, can you double check that big book you are holding to make sure my name is in there? Oh, it's not. Well then, can you see if it's under my first name or maiden name? Whew, thank goodness, I was beginning to worry."

That was the gist of my superficial relationship with God. I knew I should get back to my dedicated prayer life, but each time I would begin to pray, life would inevitably distract me, or I would go to sleep. I was spiritually weak and sick. Well, to be honest, my spiritual life was dead. I was just going through the motions. I was a bench warmer Christian. I was just taking up space on the pew, going through the motions, but not sincerely worshiping Him.

Physically, I was a shell of the person that I once was, and if I glanced at my reflection in the mirror, I would have to do a double take to confirm that the person staring back was me. I looked and moved like I inhabited the body of ninety year old woman. In addition to the classic Parkinson's tremor, I was stiff, stooped, slow, and prone to falling because my balance was so poor. Sometimes I had trouble getting my clothes on because I couldn't fasten the buttons and had trouble manipulating utensils to get food in my mouth. This angered me. Angry at myself and, though I would not admit it at the time, I was angry at my Creator. Surely He wasn't paying attention when He made me. I was thirty-seven years old and already had a living will with my final wishes in writing. I was determined to be in control of my death because I had lost control of my life.

And, the darkness of the night beckoned me for a reprieve of sorts—a time to relax and rejuvenate. The location couldn't have been more mysterious, one of the top ten haunted places in America, the Myrtles Plantation in St. Francisville,

Louisiana. Again, my mind drifted back to childhood sleepovers, where ghost stories and squealing into the wee hours of the morning was a requirement. I smiled.

My three friends and I met in the parking lot of the rural hospital where we worked as nurses. We talked and giggled as we drove towards our adventure. We stopped at a convenience store and bought our choice of alcohol for the night. Since I was not accustomed to drinking, I had no idea what to buy that I could swallow without gagging. Mike's Hard Lemonade was my choice at the suggestion of my friend Mistie. As I held the beverage in my hand, I gazed into the distance, and I thought, tonight would be a memorable experience; tonight would define the new me.

We had reserved the caretaker's cabin located outside of the main house so that we would be exempt from the curfew restrictions. We wanted to be able to roam the grounds all night. After all, if we went to sleep, we might miss the excitement, and since I needed this adventure in my life, I was not prepared to miss any of what tonight had to offer. We hastily threw our bags and ice chest in the little shotgun house and walked around taking pictures while the sun still remained, offering us brief glimpses of hope and security. We even ventured into the restaurant that was on the grounds, only to discover we couldn't even afford the appetizers, much less the main course. We giggled as we embarrassingly ordered a six dollar slice of cheesecake with a glass of water and left laughing hysterically. Country had done come to town, y'all!

We took the free tour of the downstairs area of the plantation and learned some of the history surrounding the property.

I could hear my good friend Bernette's voice in my head saying, "You don't need to be messing around that place; that place ain't nothing good." And then add, "you're gonna be brought a booger home with you. I'm telling you that I wouldn't go there if somebody gave me a million dollars!"

I smiled at the thought; she was a good friend and co-worker. She could always make me smile, even when it was inappropriate. Yet, tonight, Bernette's irrational fears of the unknown and supernatural would not keep me from taking part in this needed experience; tonight, I would make my own decisions without interference from any outside source.

I enjoyed looking at the antiques, but otherwise, I was not impressed or intrigued by any of that. I just wanted to get to the part where we had fun. We soon began drinking and laughing and strolling around in the darkness taking pictures long after the other guests were isolated in their rooms for the night. When my cell phone rang to the tune of the Twilight Zone, my friends burst into hysterical laughter. The ringtone I had chosen unknowingly would describe the realm I was about to be thrust into head first. We lit the grounds up like a swarm of lightning bugs with our flashing cameras. Our digital cameras were capturing images of orbs everywhere. I wasn't exactly sure what an orb was until someone explained that it was a circular mass of spirit energy, which was how spirits traveled. Well, they were on the move that night. I didn't care what was floating because my head was, and the night was still young. It didn't take much alcohol to produce a euphoric giddiness that I had never experienced before. I thought to myself that this was the most fun I'd had in years. As we sat on the cabin floor talking, one of my friends made the comment that I was a lot of fun when I was drunk. However, even being drunk and somewhat free did not unshackle me completely from my past.

I recall sharing with them that I was a Christian, thank you very much, and that I used to be a Sunday school teacher and had been on foreign mission trips. I told them that I had once been a Holy Roller and just look at me now, as I struggled to stand up while laughing. Looking back, those words were a slap in the face to God. I had unknowingly opened a door to a realm that few, including myself, understood. We ventured back outside and crossed over the rope that was meant to keep people off of the porch, or at least that's what the sign hanging from it implied. We rocked in the rocking chairs and continued to take pictures and giggle. I stood on the edge of the porch serenading my friends with my intoxicated impersonation of Edith Bunker; we were like kids out of school on a skip day. When we sauntered to the other end of the porch, the hair on the back of my neck stood up, and I felt a heavy, smothering pressure on my shoulders. I made a comment that we needed to move along because there was something bad there, and the look in Mistie's eyes confirmed she felt the same sense of uneasiness. On the other hand, we must not have felt too uneasy, because after the other two ladies went to sleep, Mistie and I went back to the roped-off front porch. As the orbs started appearing on our preview screens, we snapped several consecutive shots in which the orbs were not just randomly moving but purposefully moving toward or away from us. Needless to say, when the orbs were approaching, it was a strange feeling. Then simultaneously, she and I felt that looming presence again, and we turned, back to back like trained militia, in a circle, firing our cameras. Then our bravery turned into a quick retreat as we both audibly heard footsteps on the wooden porch coming towards us, and no one else was there. We ran, as if being chased, to the back porch where we sought refuge under the bright lights. Even though it was well illuminated, I still felt uneasy and frightened; so, I took a few pictures around us. Daylight emerged within minutes and the darkness faded into the destiny we had unknowingly created. We showered, ate breakfast, and loaded our bags with heavy, sand paper eyes. It had been an awesome night with friends, and I finally slept in the front seat on the way home. My sleepwalking past was over, and I was ready to emerge into a new euphoric dream of my life—one which held promise and a revitalized Joy; however, as I slept, I did not realize the hellish nightmare that loomed on the horizon.

Chapter 2

WE ARRIVED BACK AT THE PARKING LOT with as much excitement, or perhaps even more, than when we departed, and I was more excited than most to finally break free from the person I was supposed to be and to set foot into this new world of mine—into this world where I could laugh and joke and release all the burdens of my life. Strolling into the hospital, I had one thought on my mind, and that was to retell—and relive—the stories of my previous night with my friends. And, of course,   I could explain to them what an orb was. There was no reason they shouldn't be as informed as I had become. As I scrolled through the hundreds of pictures on my camera, I commented to those around that I would love to go back for another adventure; yet, studying that moment now, I realize how foolish that statement was. In that moment, the experience had awakened something within me; yet, my disturbed soul was not all that had returned from the haunting.

Still in my fog of joy, I rushed home, still as excited as before, to share the pictures with my husband. Being a bit devilish in spirit, I hoped to get a spook out of him—or at least share a laugh with him. As the pictures uploaded to my computer, I sat smiling and laughing not only at the events I had experienced but also the reaction my husband would have over those events. We needed this laughter. Yet, as I scrolled, my smile hardened and diminished quickly. The emotions I had felt were slowly retreating into a darkened place leaving me feeling cold and empty—and alone. At the picture, I stared. On the porch stood *some thing*, and I felt evil. I zoomed closer. A face appeared on my screen—a disturbing face with a slanted eye and another covered with a black patch, a strong, foreboding nose, high cheek bones, and an upside smile sneering to reveal fanged teeth, and a goatee obscured by an orb on the chin. The childish games with orbs I had envisioned for the night began to become a vicious fiend which I held tightly into the back of my mind. It was a mistake, I thought. It wasn't real. Yet, for some reason, I continued to study this image, and I convinced myself it was nothing more than the blur of bushes beside the end of the porch. And, I moved forward with the pictures. My energy levels continued to rise back to the enthusiasm I had felt previously; then, another picture revealing the same forsaken face atop an orb, floating towards me in the picture as I sat on the back porch just before daybreak enjoying a simple and relaxing rest in the rocking chair. I saw that face, and I knew it was evil. While my relationship with God wasn't as strong as it should have been, I did understand this was no angel beckoning me for salvation; instead, it was a demon summoning me to damnation.

I dialed the numbers of my friends, almost frantically, inquiring about their photos—about their images (and any unusual occurrences). Neither of them had any sightings beyond orbs and misty shadows which we attributed to ghostly figures. They had not seen this demon like I had. One forwarded me a picture which she believed could be abnormal. I studied it closely, as well, and I noticed that in this picture as I stood with two of the other ladies, a smoky fog appeared, beginning at my chest and widening and extending over my head around three to four feet, and branched out into what appeared to be three demonic images. My mind raced with questions; my heart rate intensified, and I felt an unnerving disturbance like I had never known before. Why was this just over me? Why were there faces at the top of them? What does that mean?

Chapter 3

THE NIGHT BEFORE THANKSGIVING, I tucked the older two girls in one bedroom. They were nine and six at the time. I then went to get the baby to sleep, who had just made two a couple months earlier and was talking well for her age. She kept raising her arms pleading with me to hold her. I could not resist the quiet pleas of her eyes, and like any mother, I succumbed to her wants. As I took her in my arms, she squeezed my neck tightly and pointed to the door. She frantically jumped in my arms, urging me to move towards the door. She continued this behavior for a few moments before I placed her back in her bed, and I cautiously eased towards the door. I stood outside her door listening, as I heard her quiet tears become sobs before she finally, I thought, fell into a deep sleep. I, too, was tired from the exhausting day, and I made my way to bed. The warmth and comfort of a bed can reassure a person from time to time, and I felt reassured and safe as I crawled into my bed. That security didn't last, as I was jolted awake by Joanie's shrieking screams of distress. I bolted out of bed, as fast as a person with Parkinson's could bolt, to see what was wrong. I flipped on the lights, and her face was red and streaked with tears. I grabbed her and held her tightly asking what was wrong and she wouldn't stop sobbing to talk. I glanced up at the clock; it was four thirty in the morning. An hour later, I still had a toddler clinging to my neck. She would not go to sleep and would not get back in her bed. I took her to the kitchen where she curled up on the rug by the stove as I prepared the food I was to take to my family's Thanksgiving dinner. Joanie appeared calm and happy as she sat eating her breakfast, and I broached her about the shrill sounds of the night. I asked her if she had a bad dream. She shook her head no. I asked, why she had cried, then, if she didn't have a bad dream. She finished chewing and told me the mean man woke her up.

I asked her what she talking about and she said, "The mean man, the mean man and his black dog."

I studied her face, the innocent face of my youngest daughter, and as her words fell from her mouth to my ears, I remembered the face from the orbs. The vision I had of the man in the orb, and Joanie's recital of the "mean man" could not be related, I thought. Instead, I concluded she had overheard me and my husband talking about the pictures, and she was using her own tale as a ploy for attention. Yet, even as I refused to hear her story, I continued to return to those pictures, studying them—searching for answers and clues to why and what. I became so engrossed in the pictures that I scorched my homemade baked macaroni. I would have to explain that to my family at Thanksgiving dinner, and I was hoping, as I did that, some of them could offer me some advice and some answers. While I didn't have a phone to capture the images which could be passed around from one viewer to another, I did have my voice, and I intended for someone to hear me; however, I had not counted on the reactions of some people. Most were polite enough to nod and not offer any real comment; others seemed to simply ignore me. I learned that day that you can't use the word demon around people in a serious conversation and not expect them to become uncomfortable. I offered the word up to them as if it were a sweet sin which they refused to partake by not even acknowledging or using the term. My husband, the girls, and I gathered what was left of the macaroni, and we departed. We made our way to the Christmas tree farm for the girls to pick out a live tree. It was a family tradition, and for a brief period of time, I experienced some joy again, as we all decorated the tree in the living room. Finally, the girls found exhaustion and stumbled into bed. My husband reclined in his chair watching music videos from the 90s, and I scanned more pictures. The striking of midnight came -- not only the sounds of the clock but also the sounds of my husband snoring. I snickered. The blaring of the television was not good for me or for keeping the girls asleep; so, I quietly turned off the noise and in the silence, I heard Joanie screaming again.

I found her—wet-faced, skin flushed, and sweaty. Her exasperated pleas resulted in her nearly jumping over the crib rail as I reached over to pick her up. Again, she fiercely clung to my neck. I sat in the rocking chair in her room—enjoying that rest and relaxation—and attempted to rock her back to sleep. The more I tried to calm her, the more she struggled against me. Finally, I relented, and I stood and walked around the house with Joanie in my arms, still clinging to my neck. That was the trick. She was asleep. I was tired. Just before daybreak, I heard her screaming once more. I stumbled to her bedroom, thinking only that with all her screaming and clamoring, she must be getting sick. It shouldn't have come as a surprise once more to find her in the same physical condition I had found her previously—reddened face, wet hair, tear stains, violently jumping up and down with flailing arms. I reached for her again, and I held her close to me attempting to provide her with comfort. In my arms, I asked her if she was feeling sick. Her pacifier was spit from her mouth, and I heard her speaking clearly to me:

"Mean man and black dog in here."

She repeated her phrase to me once more, pointing to the corner of the room by the curtains. I saw nothing. Again, I thought nothing more of this instance.

Night crawled back into the day again resulting in darkness and shadows on the outside and in. I carried Joanie to bed; however, she refused to enter her room. She grabbed the door facing, and began to scream, No! I struggled with her, but I finally got her inside the room, and I placed her in the crib. She remained frantic, and she refused any comforting. Instead, she grabbed onto the railings of the crib—and methodically shook them in some failed attempt to escape a prisoned hell. The closer I got to the door, the more frantic her pleas and screams became. My husband even came in to see what was wrong with her. I remained calm, assuring him that she had overheard our conversations about the pictures and was disturbed and upset. He, too, tried to console her. With her nightlight lit, we closed the door behind us, and we left her alone to cry. I left my baby alone to cry. I left her alone.

Chapter 4

EACH NIGHT WAS LIKE THE ONE BEFORE with the baby, and I was frustrated, annoyed, lonely, and scared. It had become a routine, a terror-filled, nightmarish routine. As the new year began, I hoped it would symbolize a new start for me and my family; instead, it was only just another reminder that this was not simply a dream; it was reality. In 2010, my husband and I had been embroiled in a bitter divorce proceeding, and I am ashamed to admit the amount of money we both wasted on lawyers before we realized our mistake. I had grown to despise my husband, and I did not plan to spend the rest of my pathetic, crippled life with a man who loved his herd of cows more than he loved his own family. After all, he had made the statement before that he would sell all of his cows, but, if he did that, he would be a miserable man. It only offered confirmation to me that I was, in fact, in a loveless marriage. My childhood sweetheart had broken my heart. I recounted our marriage from the early days, and I realized just how far and how fast our marriage had fallen. I searched for God in this troubled mess of a marriage which had left me unloved, unable to be healthy, and the bearer of three miscarriages. I questioned why He had allowed any of this to happen to me.

Yet, I had to push those thoughts aside as I focused on my little girl lying on the floor waiting for me to change her wet diaper. She had been easy to potty train and had been doing well until recently. As I changed her, I idly chatted with her about how she needed to be a big girl for Mommy and use the potty again. She stared at me blankly and she said, "He comin'."

I asked who she was referring to, and she simply replied, "The mean man."

I asked her where, and she leaned to the right, nodded in the direction behind me, spoke softly, almost silently, "There," and covered her eyes with her little hands.

I turned to look behind me, but I saw nothing. I asked what the mean man looked like, and she said he was purple, and I did to her what others had done to me; I convinced myself it was simply her imagination.

Wild imagination. I was thinking it must be contagious after my first encounter with a spirit. I had finally gotten the girls to sleep and taken a bath and crawled into bed. A king size bed to myself was nice sometimes. Jamie worked away from home during the weekdays, and it was hard to juggle the demands of raising three girls and not being as physically strong as I once was. The bed was my only "me" time, and that time was spent sacked out and sound asleep. This night, however, I had just gotten situated in my comatose position for the night, when I heard the door scrape across the carpet as it swung open. I raised my head and opened one eye to see which child was coming to join me in the bed. I immediately opened the other eye and focused them, then rubbed them with my knuckles. A circular ball of light was in the doorway, and there was an evil face inside, and it was staring straight ahead. I would have remembered that face for the rest of my life without ever seeing it again; it was the face from the Myrtles pictures. This ball floated through the bedroom past my bed and turned a sharp left and went into the bathroom out of sight. My heart was racing. I said out loud to myself, "Joy, ole gal, you need to get more sleep." I really thought I had just hallucinated.

A few nights later, I was asleep in my bed with the older two girls asleep beside me. I was awakened by the foot of the mattress shaking up and down as if someone were pushing down on it roughly in an attempt to wake someone up urgently. I tried to raise my head to look, but my head refused to lift from the pillow. I felt like there was a pressure over my entire body. My heart and mind were racing wildly. Slowly that same evil face with fangs drifted up from the foot of the bed and hovered right in front of my face. I don't know why I knew to say, "Leave in the name of Jesus," but I did, and the face backed up and disappeared, and I literally rolled out of the bed onto my knees. I held my tight chest, and I could feel every beat through my chest wall. I was breathing rapidly. Calm down, Joy, that was not real, that was just a very bad dream. Yeah, a bad dream. I've got to sleep more and maybe ask my neurologist if perhaps one of my Parkinson's medications can cause delusions. I laughed nervously aloud. I barely slept. I called Jamie early that next morning to tell him of my bad dream or hallucination.

Two nights later, I was so relieved Jamie was home. We both fell fast asleep out of pure exhaustion. I'm not sure why, but my eyes popped open. I lay there feeling dread and panic within. Then I started to feel that pressure moving up my legs into my waist area. I felt paralyzed. I panicked and could not speak this time, but I was able to drag my left arm from under the invisible heavy blanket and start slapping frantically at Jamie. He bolted upright in bed and felt a struggle in the bed beside him, but he didn't see anything. My arms and legs were flailing wildly. Jamie softly muttered a prayer, and the face again retreated. This time, I didn't roll out of the bed; I rolled into Jamie's arms and sobbed uncontrollably.

I finally said, through all the blubbering, "Jamie, something's in our house! My God, this is real!"

"I know it," was all he said as he held me tightly.

Chapter 5

I WAS UNSURE WHAT I SHOULD DO, what we should do now. I felt a fear I had never known—a fear that has no answer. Not only was I afraid of what I was thinking but I was also afraid of what others would think of me. I needed to talk to someone who might understand and be able to help as I analyzed my thoughts. Angela was the name that I felt God put in my head. She was the wife of our former pastor, but she and I were never close nor was she close to any of my family. However, I did know she was an avid student of the Bible, and she would provide me with a spiritual and intellectual perspective regarding my thoughts and concerns. When my husband arrived home from work, I asked him his opinion of Angela. His reply wasn't much help, and I became irritated and angry at him, and I asked again, in a more concise voice, if he thought I should call her for advice. He just shrugged his shoulders and said I guess so. What really caused me to seek her thoughts was the fact that I knew with certainty she would say exactly what she thought, whether I wanted to hear the truth or not. That is an admiral trait in a person, frank honesty. As I dialed her number, I could feel an anxiety kindling within my body and soul. The phone rang, and I waited. With each breath I took in anticipation, I had another question or thought. I worried what she would think of me; I worried she would not be able to give me any concrete advice. Then, she answered. "Hello," I said. My thoughts swirled into a chaotic cyclone of confusion.

I don't recall the entirety of our conversation. I believe I breathlessly recounted for her our tale of terror, and once again, I waited. Occasionally, she would intervene and ask questions, but I don't recall her ever indicating to me she doubted my tale. In the background, Brother Joe stood, listening to our conversation as well. I didn't mind his hearing the story from me. I did respect him as much as I did Angela, and I would accept any assistance either one of them could provide.

The phone curdled with cacophonous sounds of static in between my words and theirs, and in my annoyance at this inconvenience, I jokingly referenced a scene from an old horror movie in which the evil spirit would cause phone interference each time the desperate mother attempted to call the priest. I laughed, as did she, but we soon returned to a more serious tone and demeanor. Her voice broke the brevity of laughter, and I, after that moment of tranquility, was returned to this world haunting me. She told me of scriptures revealing the reality of demons and told me that she and her husband had discussed the topic before with foreign mission friends. She surmised the prevalence for a demonic attack occurred more outside of the United States, and after a long breath, I took some comfort in that thought.

Her voice ended, and my comfort extended as I realized she had not referred me to seek psychiatric assistance. She believed me. Her husband believed me. What I had experienced, what my family was experiencing, was not a hallucination or a nightmare indeed. It was grounded in religious text. (Ephesians 6:12) "For we wrestle not against flesh and blood, but against principalities, against powers, against the rulers of the darkness of this world, against spiritual wickedness in high places." But, my mind continued racing with questions and concerns and fears and thoughts.

Suggestions for advice, she claimed, she would seek from her missionary friends as well as getting her husband to ask some of the professors at the Baptist Seminary. Then, she offered—insisted—she wanted to pray with me. It was not until later that I realized the significance of this moment. As I sat on the floor in my baby's room, gripping the phone to my ear, I listened to Angela's prayer. The longer the prayer lasted, the more I felt I was being smothered by a rope around my chest becoming tighter. A pressure on my back forced me closer and closer to the floor—as if pushing me closer to the bowels of Hell. When the praying stopped, the pressure, the tightness, ceased as well. I paid little attention to the significance of that moment; my sole focus was relaying the information to my husband. His concern was for what to do and how to handle the situation. He looked for answers; yet, there were none I could offer at that moment. I did, however, offer to him some sign of hope. I held my baby girl closer to my chest, with her arms wrapped tightly and securely around my neck, both of us gripping the other not sure which one was in danger and which one was being the savior. For some reason, I felt an urge to sing a gospel hymn to her, in hopes of comforting her and getting her to sleep. As I sang, she cried harder and harder, her small, delicate body fighting me and the sleep. She finally relaxed in my arms, and I continued to hold her tightly until I placed her in her bed; yet, my night was not over yet. I was unable to sleep as I continued to replay the conversation of only hours before in my mind, not yet ready to accept what I feared the most.

The morning light shone into our bedroom, and I awakened with a renewed sense of hope and appreciation for life. My older girls dressed and made their way down our long driveway to await the school bus for what seemed to be a normal day of school. I, too, felt a sense of normalcy, and I took to seeking advice from an old friend. In the middle of my kitchen I turned to Him, and I offered up the questions I was fearful to ask. I called out His name, half-expecting to hear a response loudly and clearly in the stillness of the morning air. I felt disconnected from not only God but also from my own life—my own body. I was scared, fearful. I did not understand how this could be happening to me; I had done my best to be a good wife, a good mother, a good person. I had done my best to please Him, and here I stood, not myself, but fearful, scared, and while others were around, I still felt alone.

The day of brightness and hope quickly faded that night as the darkness of whatever haunted my family was not pleased with my seeking of advice and help. My husband and I brought two mattresses into our living room where he and I would stay at night with our daughters. We had to protect them. We had to. Every two hours, either my husband or I would awaken and look around the house, pray and read scripture. The effects of the lack of sleep soon became apparent as we both struggled with staying awake and focused at work; yet, we knew that in order to save ourselves and our family this was a sacrifice we must make. Now, I was struggling not only with a physical disability but also a spiritual disability. Looking at me, no longer a vibrant, healthy woman standing; instead, I looked—and felt—old and defeated.

Chapter 6

THE DAYS AND NIGHTS BLURRED QUICKLY, and there was no longer light or peace. Each moment was filled with some form of terror or deception or uncertainty. Quickly, my baby girl's mouth filled with words that did not belong to that of a child. Reiterating the "f"-word became habitual for her, no matter the times I attempted to correct her.

The first time she uttered the word to me in her childish voice, she stated, "F*** you, Mommy," and she laughed.

Being in such a state of shock, I was unsure what to do. The nightmare continued one night as she was in the bathtub and ordered me to come wash her private area, but she referred to it by a filthy slang title. Again, this was not a word that a child should be speaking; this was not a word she had heard from me or any member of our family. Within days of this, Joanie continued the madness by touching herself in vulgar, inappropriate manners. She would remove her clothing and thrust her hips suggestively; she asked about male and female genitalia. My baby girl was acting a part which she should not understand.

As Joanie continued with this type of behavior during the daytime, she fought night terrors during the darkened hours of sleep. Often times, I would overhear her in conversation with someone in her bedroom; yet, she would never enlighten me as to whom she was speaking. With Joanie seemingly becoming someone she was not, our home also began to take on a new, unearthly appearance with a haziness and fog embracing it. I even asked my husband once if our neighbors had something burning. He responded with a negative answer, and I, once again, dismissed this obvious sign of a demonic presence. Yet the behaviors continued, and when my husband returned from work the following week, I confessed all the happenings to him. He phoned a friend whom he respected, and his friend discussed our situation with his pastor and associate pastor; within hours, they had decided they would visit our home. They would rescue us from this hell on earth; our cavalry was finally arriving. I phoned Angela to entrust her with the latest development, and she warned me that spiritual warfare was no easy undertaking. Spiritual warfare, I thought, sounded beyond what I had imagined to take place; warfare was fought with swords and on battlefields which left casualties and fatalities. What I needed was simply someone to come and remove whatever was in my home, an exterminator or the terminator. My mind always found humor even in the darkest moments; it helped me stay positive or at least relieved tension. Again, she offered to pray with me on the phone and again, as she did, the pressure and tightness around me followed. There was something—or someone—in my home.

Finally, they did arrive—six members of the church who seemed just like ordinary people. I expected Hollywood-style arrival in a black car, with crosses and collars and holy water. Instead, they looked just like me or you. We sat in the living room, and while I was nervous and apprehensive about sharing this story with them, I did. I blamed myself for all my mistakes as the reasoning behind this terror. They listened intently, and one lady consoled me, explaining that I must forgive myself for I carried too much inside my soul which should not still be there. God had forgiven me, she offered. Another man, as I spoke, noticed the tremors of my disease, and he, too, offered that my illness would be cured. I laughed on the inside; yet, I offered to him a thank you. No one could cure this, I thought. The pastor and his wife led the group throughout our home, and my husband and I stayed behind. Then, I heard gibberish I had never heard before coming from around the baby's room. My husband and I moved forth, and the pastor's wife stood, in a warlike stance, seemingly prepared for battle, uttering a chant I did not know. She told us of a demon traveling towards the room, and she, in the name of the Lord, removed him from her presence. My nightmare, I foolishly thought, was over.

We all gathered in the baby's room for prayer, our arms raised to the Lord, as the pastor prayed for protection over our family—His family. I stood, praying harder than I had ever prayed before, harder than I had prayed in a long time. My prayer became more focused and more intense, and when my eyes opened, I was quick to discover the reality was I was the only one still praying. As I looked around, I saw a look on their faces I did not recognize—a deep look of concern and fear, and one of the ladies asked me if I had ever been molested as a child. I had no time to think, I simply responded affirmatively with a nod of my head. She asked what age I had been exposed to this violation, and I tentatively, almost like a child, replied with age five. She asked me if she could pray with me, and before I had time to offer another affirmative nod all three ladies had their hands placed on my head, screeching out prayers that swept through Heaven, Hell, and eternity. The pastor elaborated that the abuse question was asked because demonic spirits often latch on to sexually abused children and manifest when the victim's child grows closer to the age the abuse occurred. That, however, was not the case with me. I would not believe that.

Though, I knew in my heart the truth; I knew I had been abused by a relative at age five. I knew I had buried the pain and the shame and the guilt deep inside and refused to speak of this pain. I knew that I was not his only victim. At sixteen, I sat on my grandmother's sofa dozing between a world of reality and one of make-believe as my aunts and uncles laughed and recounted stories of their childhood. Also there that day was a brother and sister that my grandmother babysat, and they sat opposite from me on another sofa. As I heard heavy footsteps coming from the house, I happened to glance at the little girl, and I noticed—and understood—the fear in her eyes. I knew without a word from this child that she, too, was being abused by the same man who had abused me. Quickly, in her, I saw me; I was no longer sitting on that sofa; instead, I was remembering the pain, the fear that little girl felt because I was recalling the terror I had felt years before at his hands. I knew to save her, I must reveal my own hidden secret and stop his terror and to end this vicious cycle of abuse.

I did remain silent until the next day at basketball practice; I asked my coach if she had a moment to talk to me in private. With the fear inside me building to a tremble, I explained to her what had happened to me. I explained to her why I needed to reveal the truth at this moment. With her phone call to child protective services, the investigation began. My hunch was proven correct when the little girl revealed that both she and her little brother had been abused by this monster man. This revelation, however, created a whirlwind of doubt and betrayal within and among the members of my close-knit family.

On the surface, I had always belonged to the perfect American family; yet, underneath that façade, one could note how the façade would fade and reveal the skeletal remains of a family in torment and disarray. Quickly, I found that truth did not belong in this family; I was treated as the outcast because I revealed a truth that few of them wanted to admit or believe. I continued to tell my story; I continued to acknowledge the truth despite the urging from members to recant the truth. I sought help and counseling, and slowly, I began to heal my inner child.

This occurrence, I learned, was not my fault; instead, it could possibly be attributed to generational curses, the ability for demons to follow a particular family throughout generations. Demons affect families in several manners, most often being seen as mental illness such as depression, suicide, schizophrenia, bipolar disorder and addictions, such as drug or alcohol dependency. Also, they bring about physical infirmities that appear to be inherited. People, though, do not like to hear their family is cursed; instead, they argue about the possibility of demons even existing. They simply utter words like it's just in their blood, or it was born into her. The Bible states in Exodus 34:7 "keeping mercy for thousands, forgiving iniquity and transgression and sin, and that will by no means clear the guilty; visiting (punishing) the iniquity of the fathers upon the children's children, unto the third and to the fourth generation." This is beyond learned behavior, this is spiritual bondage. Many ministers and Christian leaders deny the possibility because many still believe demons cannot exist. The Bible, however, gives numerous accounts of Jesus healing by casting out demons. Consider the woman with scoliosis in Luke 13:11-13, she was said to have a spirit of infirmity. Another of many examples can be seen in Mark 9:17-26 when Jesus commanded the dumb and deaf spirit to come out of a young man. He did not merely command the illness to be gone, He commanded the spirit (demon) that was causing the illness to be gone, therefore healing the sick. I am not implying that demons are the root of all disease, many times it is merely physical and that is mentioned in the Bible as well, such as the woman with the issue of blood who was healed by merely touching His clothes in Mark 5:25-29. Also, the account of the blind man being healed by Jesus putting mud in his eyes in John 9:6&7 was not due to demonic spirits.

The group continued their claim on our home until they finally felt compelled to leave. The pastor made the statement that there was peace back in our home. His words made me question myself as they filed out the back door. Peace, I didn't feel peace. I knelt next to Joanie's baby bed and closed my eyes. I prayed silently as a tear trickled down my cheek. Joanie's screams of fear and uncertainty replayed in my mind and increased the overwhelming sense of guilt I bore. I was the reason for these unseen visitors which terrorized my toddler. This, I thought, is my fault. I clamored to God and admitted my sins and took the blame; yes, I deserved whatever punishment He wanted to hand out, but not my babies. Yet, God does not take orders from anyone, not even me with all my pleading.

Joanie's night terrors continued for days following the saving of our souls according to the group. My husband called his friend, and the pastor and his members agreed to return once more. Before their arrival, I decided I wanted the group to not only pray around our home but also to pray over my little girl. Joanie, it seemed to me, needed the prayers as well. I phoned Angela, and I confessed my worries to her. She listened, and she allowed for me to express all of my thoughts and ultimately answer my own questions. As I paced outside talking to her, the mass of fog continued to roll in over the roof of our home once more. Once our phone called ended, I found myself standing in the hallway, staring up at the string to our attic door. I reached for it and pulled on it. The attic ladder slowly appeared, and I climbed the steps one at a time until I reach the top. Once inside the attic, I reached for the light switch and flipped it on. Only the newest addition to our attic was illuminated. I demanded that, whoever or whatever was in my home, get out. This was my house! Nothing happened. There was no movement; there were no grunts or groans from any entity. I was the sole occupant of this room. Then, there was a flash I caught in my peripheral vision. A ball of light was appearing, increasing in size and structure with other lights of various colors streaming from it. I prayed louder and harder and screamed for my husband to join me. As he was climbing the stairs of the attic, the panic and fear increased in me as the ball of light began to send an appearance of fire in my direction. I urged him to retreat, and I soon followed.

He asked me what happened, and I explained the situation to him. He held me tightly; yet, I still felt neither peace or nor protection. Instead, I showered in water and tears before I phoned my best friend, Loralyn. She had this uncanny ability to understand me better than I understood myself. She knew of my current situation, and she had a faith which I trusted had been passed on to her from her parents. She told me to call her after the prayer session was over.

The two men arrived, and they and my husband laughed and chatted casually as I sat in my seat in anticipation. I needed them to do something; I needed them to rid me and my home of this terror. At last, they got up and we went into the baby's room, where she was fretfully sleeping. They laid hands on my sleeping angel and prayed. That was it. On the way to the door, my mind raced with questions and confusion and started feeling clogged as the gears became entangled with fear. I heard the words in slow motion, like an old vinyl record playing in the wrong speed , "T-h---is ----i-s---y--ou----rrr ----demon---- y-o --uuu h-a- ---v--e ----t-o ------ m--a--ke --- it ---- l---e---a---v----e." What? So, because I brought it here, I've got to make it leave? What? I was livid. Jamie followed them to the truck, laughing and talking as if they had just been on a social occasion. When Jamie came through the door, he asked, "What?"

I replied through clenched teeth, "You made me look like a crazy fool tonight!"

He asked what I meant, and I replied that he knew. He raised his voice and said that I knew he supported me. I turned to walk away, threw up my hands and said "whatever." I stormed through the house and went directly to the attic opening, pulled open the door and unfolded the ladder. I stomped up the ladder with the intention of confronting whatever evil was dwelling within. I stood in the entranceway as my heart sank in my chest. My mind was swirling so fast that I actually felt dizzy and nauseated. Jamie was standing below, looking up at me and not saying a word. It felt like I was there for minutes, though it was probably mere seconds. Tears welled in my eyes as I looked around the attic to confirm what I was seeing—a cluttered attic, just a cluttered attic. I backed down the ladder and walked to the back door, grabbing my keys off of the counter as I headed to my vehicle. I could hear Jamie speaking to me with a raised voice, but his words didn't register in my brain. I backed out and stomped the gas, causing the back of my SUV to fishtail as rocks flew. I didn't have a clue as to where I was going, but I felt like I was hurtling head long into blackness. I was sobbing so hard that I could barely see to drive. My tires kept running off the edge of the road. I was driving 70-80 mph on little one lane country roads. I was questioning my own sanity. Maybe I was crazy, maybe this had just been a figment of my imagination. I started talking aloud to someone I had been having a superficial relationship with—God. My world is falling apart, God. I don't think I can hold on much longer. God, I'd rather die now, than to face insanity. I felt like I was standing in a tunnel that was tipping, and I had nothing to hold on to so I was sliding backwards into oblivion. I picked up the phone and dialed Loralyn's number. When I heard her voice, mine cracked. "What? Joy? What happened? You ok? "The only thing I could halfway say clearly was, "They think I'm crazy!"

I was defensive and felt paranoid. The thought kept forming in my mind that Jamie was against me; everyone was against me. And creeping in like fog—the same fog that surrounded my once peaceful home—were the thoughts of "accidentally" hitting a tree. Die with dignity. No need to ruin my reputation; after all, pride and respect was engrained in my genetic makeup. Don't embarrass the family name. No one will believe you. You will stand alone. No one will back you up. You are alone. Spare your family the shame. Die with your dignity. Die. "Joy! Joy! I don't want you just driving around. Where are you? Meet me at my parents' church. I'm leaving now." Loralyn was a good friend. Jamie called several times; I didn't answer. He didn't believe me anyway.

I sat in a little country church with Loralyn, her parents, and two missionary Baptist preachers. I recounted the events that brought me to them. Their faces were solemn; I couldn't read their thoughts. Being a nurse, I was inept at reading expressions, knowing people's thoughts by looking in their eyes. When I finished speaking, I swallowed hard and stared at the floor. Loralyn's father spoke first. He always held my reverent respect. I knew when Mr. Daniel spoke, he didn't waste his breath; he spoke the truth and did so without fancy, superficial words. He simply and humbly spoke about what the Lord had done for him and how he read God's word and believed every word. I saw a side of him I had never seen before, and I was in awe at his faith. Now I knew where Loralyn obtained her solid rock foundation. This, perhaps, was the beginning of the end of this tale for me and my family. I prayed it was, even though somehow I knew it was just another beginning. We did get a few nights of peace

Until Joanie and I were wrestling on my bed one morning after the other two left for school and we simultaneously heard clicking footsteps coming from the direction of the kitchen. From our position on the bed, we saw a dark silhouette dart into Joanie's room. She looked at me with fear and asked, "Who was dat?" I told her it was nobody, but I knew it was the demon with a human-like body and hooved feet. Lord, why is this nightmare torturing my life?

Chapter 7

JAMIE'S OLDER BROTHER WAS DISTURBED by the thought of a demon scaring the girls. He told us that he had dated a girl in the past who could communicate with demons. He said she could see and smell them as well. He had located her and shared with her our situation. She felt compelled to help us because children were involved. The sun was shining outside the afternoon my brother –in-law's truck pulled into the drive. The two older girls were in school and Jamie and I were home with little Joanie. I was skeptical as I watched the woman slowly get out of the truck. She wasn't much over five feet tall, pale, and could not possibly weigh more than one hundred pounds soaking wet. The biggest thing about her was her hair; it was wavy and wildly sticking out in every direction. The word psychic never came to mind, I was so ignorant. That was one of the many, many mistakes that I made. It was my wave-the-magic-wand-and-make-it-disappear theory. I soon came to realize that the Bible held warnings regarding psychics. In Leviticus 19:31, it states: Regard not them that have familiar spirits, neither seek after wizards, to be defiled by them: I am the Lord your God.

She introduced herself and talked briefly, saying she felt the evil within when she was about three miles from my house. She was wringing her hands and her eyes were darting all around. She asked if she could go inside alone and talk to him. I closed the door behind as I walked outside under the garage with Jamie, Travis and little Joanie. We made small talk as Joanie road her tricycle in circles. Slow waves of rotten stench kept enveloping my senses to the degree I could taste it. My chest felt tight, I felt like I was smothering, but I thought it was from that atrocious odor. I realized that while I was struggling to maintain my composure, Joanie had gotten off her bike and was walking around acting scared. She came up to me and hugged my leg and said she was ready to go. I asked where she was ready to go.She replied, "'Way from dis stinkin' place!"

The 'demon-whisperer,' what I had sarcastically named her, told us that we had a spirit from the Myrtles Plantation with his dog and said the dog liked the baby. My thought was, as I laughed to myself, then why is she terrified? Also, she said, there was a dominant spirit that was controlling the other spirits and keeping them at our house against their will. My goodness, spirits are bullies too, wow. While we were standing in the driveway, the demon-whisperer started acting nervous, jittery, with darting eyes. I asked if she was okay. Then as fast as a streaking nun, she ran to the back door and slammed it shut. She looked at me with her finger pointing as she got in my face and told me NOT to let him out because he would gain more strength from the spirits outside. Keep the door shut? What? Can't spirits go through walls? They did on Scooby-Doo anyway.

Jamie and I arranged for the kids to spend the night with his mom, and we stayed up cleaning up the house, doing the laundry, and finally relaxing and discussing our questions about what was about to take place. This demon chic said she would return at 3 a.m. because this was the opposite of 3 p.m. when Jesus died on the cross. She stated spirits were generally more active at this time. Neither of us prayed, nor did we refer to the Bible for answers. We just sat numbly and waited. As headlights shined through the living room window, our thoughts were jolted back towards anxious concerns and questionable hopes. The back door burst open as the wild-eyed demon lady returned, wearing old fashioned slip-on house slippers and two hands wielding grocery store sage. We scrambled around to accommodate her with saucers and bowls in which to burn the sage. I inquired of her the exact purpose behind the sage, because I knew nothing about the practice. She explained that it is a powerful spiritual cleansing technique which calls upon the spirits of various sacred plants to drive away negative energy and to restore balance to an individual, a group, a space, or all three. This tradition has been a part of the spirituality of Native Americans for thousands of years. As the smoke trail started creeping around like a dense fog, she moved purposefully to all four corners of every room carrying the smoking sage and fanning it into the air. She asked Jamie to read scripture out loud throughout the house. He did as she said, and I was astounded. He read like it was second-nature to him; I was listening to the next Jimmy Swaggart. I was impressed, but it apparently irritated the demon. I recall a bowl of sage shattering as Jamie left Joanie's room. I would have credited this little explosion to the heat from the smoking sage, but no other bowl shattered that night, and this was the exact spot that my rear end had been scratched as I exited that same bedroom door just a couple of weeks prior. Obviously, Joanie's room was this thing's territory, and it didn't want God's word in its territory. The day I was scratched, Jamie and I were walking around reading scripture. I was reading from the Book of Hebrews, chapter 9:14: "How much more shall the blood of Christ, who through the eternal spirit offered himself without spot, to purge your conscience from dead works to serve the living God." It didn't take me long to figure out that this entity did not want to hear anything about the blood of Jesus. It made this thing very angry. As I exited Joanie's room behind Jamie, I felt a stinging sensation to my right hip/buttocks area. I compared the feeling much like when as a child, my older brother would roll up a dish towel and snap it hard at me, and it would make a loud cracking noise and would sting like fire if it made contact. It seemed that the stinging sensation intensified as we continued our mission to make this thing leave. I stopped in front of the bathroom mirror and unbuckled my belt and slipped my jeans down enough to inspect the stinging area. I immediately yelled for Jamie to come look. To our horror and disbelief, there were three angry, red, raised welts on the top of my right butt cheek. "My God," Jamie said, "when did this happen?"

I replied by adding my own question, "How did it scratch me through my jeans and not make a sign or tear them?" We were both feeling the same horrified sense of fear of the unknown, and at the same time, the anger intensified because something was in our house acting as if it had authority and had the audacity to harm us at will.

I reminded myself what Angela had said on many occasions, "Satan and his demons are like a pit bull on a chain. They can't take your life, they are not allowed, God will jerk the chain. Therefore, there are boundaries and rules Satan himself has to follow. The ultimate reality is that God controls everything in the universe, including Satan."

I was thinking and wondering why God didn't just say, No and end our nightmare. I learned that Satan has a vested interest in keeping everyone ignorant about his mode of operation. His ultimate victory is for people, especially Christians, to believe that he doesn't really exist. That very idea, that he is just a Biblical fairy-tale character leaves the proverbial door to our lives wide open and invites trouble, trials, and anguish that we just can't seem to understand the source of our misery. I realized that this was true for everyone, good or bad, and that the suffering we experience is no indication of our sinfulness or our godliness. I can't tell you how many times I was asked if I was sure I was a Christian believer. I learned to recite a verse from Romans 8:38-39: "For I am persuaded, that neither death, nor life, nor angels, nor principalities, nor powers, nor things present, nor things to come, nor height, nor depth, nor any other creature, shall be able to separate us from the love of God, which is in Christ Jesus our Lord." My personal thoughts were why would Satan benefit from tormenting a lost person? He already has claim to their soul, but a Christian on the other hand, can be tormented and tortured to the point of falling from grace and destroying their witness. That would put a stumbling block in the path of many lost people that would prevent them from ever having a relationship with God.

Once the bowl exploded, the side-show began. We watched as she went throughout the house sucking the spirits into her body, then going outside to get down on all fours, contort, twist, and growl while expelling the spirit out of her into the night. This is nuts, I thought to myself as I watched her go in and out, back and forth, countless times. Once, she came up to me and was huffing and puffing in my face saying that she stopped counting at 48. Forty eight minutes? I asked, because it had nearly gone on for an hour. "No, forty-eight spirits," she replied as she staggered like a drunk. She said she was weak, but she was about to take out the big dog. She asked if I had any baby powder. Sure, why, I replied. Just go get it, I was told. She proceeded to shake that powder out onto my clean kitchen floor in a large circle. She instructed me to get my Bible and get in the circle. She explained that it would protect me because the entity would attack me on the way out if I didn't do what she said. Honestly, I wasn't worried about being attacked by a demon. My obsessive-compulsive nature had me staring at the powdered mess on my freshly mopped kitchen floor. I was livid, literally, at the ridiculousness of these shenanigans. Nevertheless, I regained enough composure to hold my Bible and kneel to pray. First, she knelt down about six feet in front of me, directly outside of Joanie's room. She started speaking another language and speaking as if engaged in a serious conversation with someone. She began to convulse on the floor; yet, somehow, amidst the convulsions, she told Travis that she was too weak to get up, that he must carry her outside. I watched him strain, red faced, to scoop her up and carry her outside. My Lord, I thought, I hope he doesn't fall with her or have a heart attack because I've got to stay in this circle of baby powder that has messed up my floor. I smiled at my ability to still find humor in the darkest situations. Back and forth they went, taking out the trash so to speak, until I finally sat down in my circle and watched like a spectator at a tennis match. Then she went to the attic entrance and stood there looking up. The maniacal look in her eyes alarmed my innermost composure. I stood up. From where I was in the kitchen, I could see through the bathroom (which had a door on each end) into the back hallway. I watched as her thin, feeble frame climbed the ladder into the dark uncertainty. Jamie was reading from the Book of Psalms, with a loud, booming voice that resonated throughout the house; yet, my ears were consumed with a repetitive sound that I soon recognized as my own voice repeating the fourth verse of the Twenty-third Psalm—"Yea, though I walk through the valley of the shadow of death, I will fear no evil: for thou art with me; thy rod and thy staff they comfort me." As Travis stood beneath the attic entrance, he turned and looked at me. I could see fear in his eyes. There was a change in the air around us, as if the atmosphere was a deflating balloon, and the air was being ripped away from our bodies. I felt smothered; I struggled to take a deep breath. When I looked toward Travis, it was as if an opaque sheet of glass was between us, which then distorted into a fun house mirror image of him as he ran toward me with a limp body cradled in his arms. It felt as if the air was being pulled out as he went through the back door; the force nearly made me tip forward out of my circle. The baby powder was even blown forward on the floor. Jamie ran out behind them. I didn't know if I was supposed to leave my supposed sanctuary or not, so I elected to stay. I got down on my knees and said aloud, "They left me. Here I am alone; now what?Still talking to myself, I said,

"No, I'm not alone. God, you are still here."

I opened the Bible with my sweaty hands and read Psalm 121—"I will lift up mine eyes unto the hills, from whence cometh my help. My help cometh from the Lord, which made the Heaven and Earth. He will not suffer thy foot to be moved; he that keepeth thee will not slumber. Behold, he that keepeth Israel shall neither slumber nor sleep. The Lord is thy keeper: the Lord is thy shade upon thy right hand. The sun shall not smite thee by day, nor the moon by night. The Lord shall preserve thee from all evil; He shall preserve thy soul. The Lord shall preserve thy going out and thy coming in from this time forth, and even forever more."

As I read this, I could hear animal-like growling, snarling, and howling. Jamie later told me that was the demon-slayer releasing the big dog spirit. The whole block was disturbed. Cows were not just mooing, they were bellowing; numerous neighborhood dogs were barking and howling; coyotes were yelping. Jamie also said our usually docile English bulldog nearly attacked her as she flopped on the ground. The sounds gradually subsided, and then my senses were plunged into total silence except for the clock ticking. I sat there until my legs had a pins and needle sensation; I deemed it safe to leave my circle. Just then, Travis entered with the demon catcher unconscious in his arms. She looked dead. He laid her limp body on the couch, and we all collapsed in the living room as well. We sat in silence, each consumed in our thoughts of the dreamlike or should I say nightmare-like events replaying in our minds. She slept for nearly two hours as I swept and mopped the floor. I had to have cleanliness and order, or I just could not think clearly. I cooked a pile of French toast, bacon and eggs for everyone. At the table, sleeping beauty ate like a stray dog and talked nonstop. Occasionally, she would turn and have a conversation with someone that none of us could see. She said it was her spirit guide. Normally, I would have had to stifle my laughter, but I was too exhausted. She assured me every single spirit had been freed, and I could rest easy.

She spoke, "In Matthew 12:45 it says 'When the unclean spirit is gone out of a man, he walketh through dry places, seeking rest; and finding none, he saith, I will return unto my house whence I came out. And when he cometh, he findeth it swept and garnished. Then goeth he and taketh to him seven other spirits more wicked than himself; and they enter in and dwell there: and the last state of that man is worse than the first.'" She asked if I knew what that meant.

I looked at her and said, "So, I shouldn't have cleaned up the mess on the floor?"

She obviously didn't care for my sarcasm. She pointed a shaky finger in my face and told me I must never doubt that they were all gone. A few minutes later in the living room, a familiar and foreboding scent filled my nose. .I hesitated for a minute until I had to break the silence and say, "I smelled it, it's still here."

She waved a hand at me to dismiss that notion and explained that was just the "after smell." I sat there wanting to sarcastically reply to that word that I really wasn't sure was even a word. I kept silent and tried to dismiss my gut instincts. Then she started talking again to something I couldn't see. Saying, you are welcome, sweetie and thank you. She answered the question in my eyes. "I'm talking to the children, the children he was holding captive here."

Dear Lord in Heaven, she is insane; I almost muttered that aloud. I looked at Jamie as she drifted into sleep again and rolled my eyes. Travis had dozed off again at the opposite end of the couch; so, Jamie and I lay down in our bedroom. I was numb with exhaustion as my eyelids opened and shut in a slow motion. I felt startled twice, and my eyes flew open and darted anxiously around the room. I took a deep sighing breath both times, relieved that I saw nothing unusual. Then about thirty minutes into my brief refuge of sleep, my blurred eyes opened and scanned my surroundings again. Oh no, the blurriness cleared instantly, and he was back—there was that darn demonic face.

I foolishly recall making the statement that it couldn't get much worse. I will never speak those words again in any situation. I wasn't sure what the psycho psychic had done, but our little two-man sideshow had grown overnight into a huge three-ring circus. We were infested with spirits; there were too many to count and no two looked alike. The haze-like fog was throughout the house. It was literally stifling, hard to breath. This was not good. I noticed the dark shadows that once hovered in the corner of the room were now appearing to be inside the walls themselves. I started taking pictures and videoing to document what I was seeing. In the beginning, the images were nothing more than what appeared to be a blurry or dark picture, but with time, the entities were well-defined. Taking pictures was not good as I was told, but if this provided evidence that neither I, nor my children, were crazy, then so be it.

I was still sailing in regards to income, on my short-term disability benefits, but it was not enough. Jamie had burned his bridges by resigning from his job without notice. He stayed home for two months before he had no choice but to resume his career on the road. I tried not to let him know how desperately I needed to hide behind him. By now, the interaction between my two-year-old and one of the spirits intensified. She spoke about a black dog frequently and I tried to hold on to the hope that she was just making reference to the neighbor's dog that wandered into our yard on occasion. Jamie was becoming agitated and angry. He felt helpless. Many times, he would witness Joanie being startled by something he could not physically see, and she would run away screaming or just sit and cover her eyes while screaming. On the other hand, Joanie could be defiant and merely laugh in mockery if we reprimanded her in any fashion. Then at bedtime, it was the same old song and dance of fear and anxiety. These emotions rubbed off on her older sisters, as they began to clearly see the same things that Joanie and I were seeing. The entire household was in a state of chaos. Sometimes at night Jamie would become enraged at the fear that was being evoked throughout his family. He would rant and rage loudly at something that he couldn't even see. He realized that was the tactic the devil used to attack his mind. Jamie would scream, "Show yourself to me!" He would beat his chest with his fists much like King Kong. Sometimes I would envision Jamie literally wrestling with a demonic spirit and it made me smile to myself.

OK, so now what? I knew this was a very serious situation; I admitted it as I discussed our predicament with my cousin Rachel. We often sought refuge at Rachel's house, crashing there for a two or three night reprieve. She told me that I needed to talk to Brother Garcia at the local Pentecostal church. She said he had experience with this before and would surely be willing to help us. I contacted the pastor's wife, Suzonne, and they soon were sitting on my couch, listening as I recounted as many details as I could recall. They both had a serious look of concern in their eyes, but Bro Garcia's eyes held a look that made me feel angry and defensive: pity. That was the last thing I wanted; sympathy from him, or anyone for that matter.

When I finished talking, he said, "So you can see them, Sister Joy?" I nodded yes. He asked me to show him where one was at that moment, so I glanced around and saw one hovering under the dining room light. Bro Garcia walked casually to the place I pointed and waved his hand and arm right through it. He couldn't see it, but he said it was right in front of him because he could smell it. Before I was even aware of the trespassers in our home, I would notice the smell of rotten eggs or spoiled meat. I would spray air freshener, unaware of the source of the odor. When Bro Garcia said he smelled it, I was so relieved that I was not the only one aware that demons have an odor.

We sat around the dining room table, reading scripture and praying. I recall reading 1Peter 5:8. "Be sober, be vigilant; because your adversary the devil, as a roaring lion, walketh about, seeking whom he may devour." Until that moment, I had never understood the depth of that verse. I was distracted, however, by the movement of black, and sometimes white, masses that were purposefully moving back and forth across the top of the wall. A lot of times, though, they were stationary under the light fixtures for hours. Later, I learned that was how spirits gained strength through electrical energy. We would notice surges in the power that caused the light to fluctuate from bright to dim and it made the egg-shell-white walls to appear yellow or orange. I documented the phenomena by taking many consecutive pictures of the changing wall colors. The steep increase in our electricity bill was evidence that something was consuming more energy than usual. I set up my own video surveillance and noted that the black mass would slink from the closets or from behind the beds and it appeared as a swarm of bees or a black tornado. While we slept, this ominous darkness would move around us, enveloping our entire bodies. Later, I also learned that was how they obtained energy or the strength to move about and manifest into forms or faces.

Bro Garcia, Suzonne,, Jamie and I went throughout the house praying. Bro Garcia sternly commanded the spirits to leave, but instead, they ran like a chicken from a fox through and around the walls, from room to room. Finally, we called it a night and actually slept pretty well for two nights. Did I think they were gone? Nope. I could feel them in the air. It was a heaviness or a thickness to the air itself. I felt like they were hiding from the fresh anointing oil around the house. Bro Garcia did continue to return for prayer and then requested to stay in our home alone overnight and sleep in Joanie's room. I was shocked at his determination, but I was sure of one thing, nothing would happen out of the ordinary. These spiritual beings were intelligent and always retreated when a man of God came as if they were threatened by the spirit within the man. Bro Garcia stayed one night as promised, and I was disappointed, yet not surprised, when he called and said nothing happened. Even though that was what I had expected, I felt something was telling me that Bro Garcia thought it was all in my head too, that I was crazy. My own father had recently told me it was just me imagining thing, that I was crazy and Bro Garcia was too if he believed me. My father even called Loralyn's father, Mr. Daniel, and questioned him. Mr. Daniel told him that the Bible had account after account of the existence of demons AND God as stated in James 2:19: "Thou believest that there is one God; thou doest well: the devils also believe and tremble." My father didn't believe in God as far as I knew, so I understood why he didn't believe in demons. But it angered me when he said such hurtful things to me, but also saddened me to know his state of mind or to know the state of his soul.

Chapter 8

IT BECAME OBVIOUS THAT MOST BAPTISTS don't really think demons are real or that appearing in someone's home to torment their family was their mode of operation in present day. While I am able to laugh at that thought now, during this battle of faith, I began to question not only myself but also the foundation of my beliefs. We were hesitant to even disclose our plight, but I was in desperate need of all the prayer I could solicit, so I swallowed hard and dialed my Sunday school teacher. Mr. Charlie was someone I admired greatly. He not only talked the talk, he walked the walk. He may not have understood exactly what was happening, but he believed me. Once our Baptist church found out, I believe the congregation was evenly divided as to the believers and the non-believers. A handful believed; a handful didn't, and a bigger handful believed, but they were scared to admit it. They presented us with a check for a large sum of money, and we appreciated the gesture greatly. However, later, we thought about it and wondered if perhaps we should have offered it to the demons to make them leave. We tried not to be sarcastic, but the little humor we could find in the situation was perhaps what mostly kept us with some sanity at all. Our church had told us they were going to start a prayer vigil and circle around the outside of our home and pray each night until this ended. However, no one showed up; they decided they could just pray from the church instead. That hurt. We soon realized that most of the ones who were sending "praying for you" cards were actually praying for my mental health.

Inside the house, there were still night terrors for Joanie, even though she slept with me. She would cry and cover her eyes. I would continuously notice her talking to herself, and often I would find her with her clothes off, lying in vulgar positions. I didn't understand what was going on with her. We stayed at my mother-in-law's house frequently where we would camp out in her living room. The kids felt safer there, and they felt like they could relax without having to worry about what they might say that they shouldn't. My mother-in-law was just absolutely a God-send. The girls could talk openly about the things we were experiencing, and she listened and believed. The girls felt uncomfortable staying anywhere else because they were told that it was not real; they were told that their mommy was just sick and putting thoughts in their heads. It made them question their own sanity, especially my nine-year-old. Her self-esteem was already low; this was an added blow to her insecurities.

We had sought help from a Non-Denominational church, Missionary Baptist, Baptist and a Pentecostal church, but didn't all the old horror movies use a priest? Through a former co-worker, who was Catholic, I was able to contact a priest from New Orleans. He came one afternoon with a local parishioner. We talked briefly; they recited a prayer and began walking through the house reciting prayers and sprinkling holy water in each room. The older girls were in school; so, Joanie was home with me. I did not tell the priest what I was seeing, but if the holy water accidentally landed upon the black fog area, literal bright sparks were flying from the wall.

I knew Joanie saw this too when I heard her say, "Oooh, look, fire crackers, Mommy."

The priest had no idea what she meant, and I dared not to elaborate; I just wanted the spirits to leave. When we made it to the back bedroom that was my oldest daughter's' Joanie spoke up and said, he was in the corner, and the priest turned to walk out as if he didn't hear her.

"She just said he's in that corner, did you hear her?" "Yes, ma'm," he replied as he literally slung the holy water from over half-way across the room and hastily recited a prayer.

He was sweating when he was done. He told me to sprinkle salt around the house, window seals, and doorways. I asked what would that do, and he replied that they can't or don't like to cross the salt. I thought this was a novel idea; however, I had some doubts about how much this might help. I likened it to putting snake-away around your house, but, I thought, if the snake is already under or in your house, then… it won't leave, right? So if these spirits didn't leave, I said, and I knew they didn't, then we keep our house guests, right? I hated to be sarcastic, but this was not working. He said to call him if it didn't help; so, I replied that I'd be in touch…soon.

Within two weeks I called back. Joanie still had ridiculous sleep disturbances. I was angry, and I was scared. Fear and anger, as I later learned, made demonic spirits more powerful; that was gourmet food to them. The priest informed me that an exorcism of the house itself was required, but there was only one exorcist per archdiocese, and he was booked. With exorcisms, I wondered. Perhaps this occurrence was even more common than I thought. But the same priest came back with the exorcist, and they kissed their purple collars that they had around their necks, and they adorned themselves in long, black robes. The exorcist recited a prayer in Latin. The air in the house tightened around me, and I felt smothered. Black shadows darted not only in the walls but also out of the walls, swooping down like birds after prey. I was thinking I was glad Joanie wasn't here to see this. As the priest and his booming, commanding voice went through the house, I followed behind. Those swooping figures were flying through me and sometimes caused me to stagger. Then I felt hands grabbing my legs and arms, and each step was a struggle to pick each foot up to take a step. By the time he got to the master bedroom, I looked in and although it was 2:30 in the afternoon and a bright, sunshiny day and the curtains were open, our room was black. I took two steps backward and told him I couldn't go in there. While that room was prayed over, I turned and staggered back through the house and out the back door. It was hot outside, humid with no breeze, but I took two gasping breaths, and I could breathe better than I could inside with the air conditioner on 64 degrees. They said good-bye, and they drove off as I stood bent at a 90 degree angle, clutching my chest. I dropped to my knees in the grass beside the driveway, and I was forcefully shoved from behind in between my shoulder blades right into the grass on my face. The sun was still shining, but there was a shadow darkening the area where I was face down. I glanced around with the one eye that was not smashed in the grass. I noticed the grass was getting shaggy, and there were many small pieces of wrappers, napkins, and broken doll pieces scattered around. My words, I had let my yard get trashy. That is how I cope, to think thoughts of uselessness. I knew the drill by now, something didn't want me on my knees praying because I just might rebuild a renewed relationship with my Heavenly Father. I recited Isaiah 43:2 that I'd recently memorized: When thou passest through the waters, I will be with thee; and through the rivers, they shall not overflow thee: when thou walkest through the fire, thou shall not be burned; neither shall the flame kindle upon thee." I knew God was with me; so, I thought, why can't I feel you? I was released in a matter of minutes, but it sure seemed like forever to me. God, I prayed, is this ever going to end?

Chapter 9

I QUESTIONED JOANIE A NUMBER OF TIMES, trying to determine with whom or what she was conversing. I tried to keep in mind, that despite the fact she was fluently talking, she was only two years old. One morning, after getting the older girls on the bus, I got the idea that I would place my cell phone close to Joanie and record what she was saying. I figured that if I could hear what she was saying, then I could determine what it was saying to her. That morning, Joanie was lying on my bed in my room, while I was in the adjoining bathroom getting ready to run errands. I was in and out, interacting with her because she wanted me to lie down beside her on the bed. I only sat momentarily though. She asked for cereal for breakfast; so, she followed me to the kitchen, I fixed her a bowl, placed the recording cell phone nearby and went to get my clothes for the day. It wasn't until after lunch that I got a chance to listen to the recorded audio. I was driving home from Walmart, and Joanie was snoozing in her car seat in the back. As I listened, my head began to spin, and my heart began to twist. Emotions mixed. Disbelief of what I was hearing swirled inside my head as sheer terror gripped my heart. My baby wasn't just talking to herself; a male voice was talking, as well. I forwarded this clip to a couple of friends to see if they heard it too. They did. This audio absolutely confirmed that this was a desperate situation. The first clip was recorded in my bedroom; that voice hissed and snarled anytime I entered the room. It was even answering the questions that I was asking Joanie. Before we went to the dining room, I could hear her talking and softly singing. This little song she sang in her innocent little angelic voice broke my heart. "Light out, he near me, lights out, keep the light on, man out there." I had to stop on the side of interstate and sob. Sobbing overcame me because Joanie had asked me repeatedly to lie down. She never said that something was in the room beckoning her to leave with it or him. I felt immense guilt resulting in a physical pressure and pain in my chest. I was always too busy to stop and just sit and enjoy my children. They were my gift from God, and I was too busy to lie down with her for five minutes.

Then I listened to the dining room clip. Joanie made noises banging her spoon on her bowl, but when I turned up the volume, I knew why. She was trying to drown out the monster's voice. With each bang of the spoon, he was saying "Stop it, stop it, stop it!" He called her name in a stern, demanding voice. Then she paused the banging long enough for him to say, "Get up, get up and come suck it!" Quickly the banging resumed, and the thing was evidently annoyed because it said, "Son of a bi***!" Then Joanie piped up and said, "Don't say bi***!"

I had a good pity party the remainder of the day. Look what I brought here. It was my fault. I lashed out at God again.

"God, why are you allowing my innocent children to be terrorized?"

"Why don't you just punish me?"

"Oh, forget it, you obviously don't hear my prayers anymore."

After that day, my home was a battleground of torment and despair. This was war; nobody or no demon was going to talk like that to my babies.

Chapter 10

I WAS TRYING TO BE LOGICAL, looking for someone who was qualified to make these evil spirits leave. Repeatedly, I felt like religion had let me down. Time to go another route, I thought. I was desperate. By this time, all three girls were terrified at night. Joanie was heavily influenced by something she apparently could see better or clearer than I could. I would restlessly doze off on the couch, while the kids slept on pallets of quilts on the floor. I placed crucifixes and open Bibles around them. I placed crosses on a chain around their necks. The walls were gleaming with blessed oil and holy water. By this time, I was sleeping around four hours a night. The girls would be close to midnight each night going to bed, and it showed in their little weary eyes when they had to go to school. They didn't deserve this. I felt like I had brought this here. This was a nightmare, and I had caused it. My God in Heaven, why do my children have to suffer because of my sins? Generational curses? Hmmmm, now I was beginning to see how this spiritual world the Bible so frequently refers to in scripture works. Not only did I see how it worked, but I could really feel it, and I didn't like it.

I didn't like it one bit, because it wasn't normal. It placed a divide between my parents and me. Forsaken. I had never felt forsaken before. I never really had an idea how that must feel. I always think of Jesus dying on the cross when He felt forsaken by God as He bore the weight of sin. I had told my parents bits and pieces, but I kept most of the details private. I knew that they would never be able to absorb the enormity nor depth of our situation. But I never fathomed the divide that would result from their disbelief. I loved my parents deeply, but my back was against the wall, and I felt each staggering blow from the bricks they were throwing at me. They were supposed to be my leaning post, my security, and now, it seemed I was a rapidly deflating balloon, bouncing from wall to wall and then collapsing. I felt alone despite the support my husband provided. I felt very alone and frankly, I was terrified. It publicly discredited me that my own parents said I was hallucinating. I could tell whom they had influenced by the way they spoke to me. If someone looked at me with pity, gently patted my arm and in the tone you would address a toddler say, Hey honey, how are you feeling, hmmm? Better? Good! (They always seemed to answer as if I were not capable or either they did not want to hear my reply).

I had to be physically doing something to keep my sanity. If I had just sat around with my thoughts, I would have allowed depression to capture me. Honestly, I have never been depressed. Because Parkinson's disease causes a flat affect, or no facial expression, it was often assumed that I was in a deeply depressed state. What people didn't realize was that even when I was extremely happy, it took a tremendous, focused effort to make the muscles in my face tighten into a smile. If I glanced at a reflection of myself during laughter, my face appeared stiff and forced; I noticed myself at times with the appearance of a mannequin. I recall telling an opinionated neighbor who seemed to think she knew more about my mental state than I, that if I were depressed, I would have been dead a long time ago. To avoid such a state of mind, I painted cabinets and walls, tiled bathroom floors, designed and built a 1,500 piece paver patio, built the kids a wooden outdoor playhouse, just whatever I could do to preoccupy my mind. My mother thought my involvement in these projects was causing the neglect of my children. It appeared that way because if she dropped in unexpectedly, I purposefully avoided contact by immersing myself into work. I came through one night, and she had Jamie cornered telling him I needed psychiatric help, that he should have me committed. I walked away more numb than ever. My family physician informed me that she called just about every day for a two-three week period, trying to get past the clerk. She wanted Dr. Magee to do an MRI of my brain to check for a brain tumor, then again, perhaps he could have me placed somewhere for psychiatric treatment. Thankfully, Dr. Magee knew me well enough to realize that I was not exhibiting any psychiatric symptoms. His unwavering support meant the world to me because not only was he a colleague at the hospital but he was also a friend. I was deeply hurt by my mother's determination to get me help that I didn't need. What I needed was her shoulder to cry on, her arms to hold me as my world crashed around me, to tell me it was going to be okay. I would soon come to realize why this separation had to occur. God had to break my dependence on anyone but Him. I found a comforting verse that I would repeat often to keep myself from grieving over the lost relationship with my parents, Psalm 27:10: "When my father and my mother forsake me, then the LORD will take me up." I knew they thought they were doing the best thing, but they had no clue.

In regards to looking beyond religion, I started from the beginning, looking at the situation from a scientific standpoint. I knew that Jamie and I both had unexplained auditory experiences in the house since the day we moved there. We definitely felt the presence of a male spirit because of the heavy footsteps. These footsteps exemplified one with authority, with long rhythmic strides. Neither of us feared what we were hearing, actually, we joked about our ghost that walked around, rummaging through unseen drawers. I was not frightened to stay there alone while Jamie was away. When we remodeled and added onto the house, which had been built in 1943, the construction workers felt uneasy there, but we never prodded for specific stories.   So, I figured to track down a previous resident and question them of any unusual problems. I ended up talking to a man who was raised in that house who now lives in Alabama. No, nothing, but he believed me, and he and his wife wanted to help. Mike and Linda were so sincerely sweet and immediately went to work searching for someone to help us. They got in touch with a paranormal group from south Mississippi, who immediately called. This group of ladies planned to come to our home within two weeks. The activity with Joanie intensified. Neither she nor I got any rest. She was talking with this unseen intruder and acted as if it were a playmate. Yet, at night, the terror continued without invitation. I had stood about as much chaos as I could endure, or so I thought. Looking back, I can say that was just the beginning of true madness. I picked up the phone in the kitchen and looked through a pile of bills on the counter, looking for the number for one of the ladies from the paranormal group. Joanie was standing in front of me, asking for a snack, her face still red and splotchy from the recent encounter with the mean man. As I dialed the number, to my disbelief and horror, Joanie went hurtling forward about four feet in front of me onto the floor. Crying ensued again. I knelt down to comfort her and make sure she wasn't hurt. I asked her if she tripped, she shook her head no.

She pointed behind me and said, "He pushed me!"

I turned and looked, but I could only see a blurry mass hovering in the corner. I scooped my baby up and took her to the living room, where I was able to proceed with my phone call. I explained what had just happened, and to my surprise, she said that it was very typical for a spirit to become aggressive when it knew someone was coming to help. I could have done without knowing that information. Now I had to be that much more vigilant. I intended to protect my girls and give them security, no matter the cost to me.

The paranormal group was made up of women, and the first time they came to our home, they seemed to be the answer. They were aware there was activity in our home and agreed to come back. Before leaving they burned sage and did a smudging of our home; the founder of the group could see what I saw and that did make me feel somewhat better. When they returned for an all-night investigation, the founder appeared annoyed and distracted. She told me that I needed to learn to live in harmony with the spirit world. Harmony? Live in harmony with a supernatural intruder that was terrifying my children and torturing me? That was the most absurd, ludicrous notion I had ever heard. At first I laughed, then, I was downright furious. My children and I spent the night with my mother-in-law, and Jamie hung around with one suspicious eye on the investigators. They were monitoring their cameras remotely from the garage. Jamie stood outside the garage window smoking. All activity was minimal, which was expected when outsiders were present. This tactic was used to discredit our claims. One sure thing was certain; these things were clever, intelligent beings. They were capable of interfering with phone communication and speaking through the phone if they so desired. I also have no doubt they knew what I was texting and what I was reading on the computer. I would not research anything pertaining to the subject of demons. Actually, if I stayed in one place for more than five to ten minutes, the dark fog would envelope my head and cause me to feel drugged, lethargic and somewhat disoriented. I couldn't even focus my eyes. The same thing would occur if I attempted to read the Bible. I would write Bible verses down on index cards or sticky notes and leave them hidden throughout the house. That way, when I was faced with the enemy, I always had God's word close at hand. I tried to recite scripture verses that I knew when trying to annoy the demons to leave, but they would advance toward me and fear crept upon me. I would stutter and stammer and then my mind would just go blank. Obviously, my plan was not effective warfare tactics.

In the wee hours of the morning, Jamie was still hanging around waiting for the team to wrap things up when he overheard the investigators discussing the sale of voodoo dolls as a means to make money. That was the final straw for him; he asked them to pack up and leave. The very next morning when we walked through the back door, I could feel a change in the air. It was heavy pressure, but it was different than it had been. The air actually felt like static electricity; it felt prickly all over. When I entered Joanie's room to put the girls' overnight bags down, something streaked from the ceiling area to the floor. It looked like streaks of light and sparks similar to fireworks. Here we go again, now they are really mad. Just as I thought, these spirits tormented the entire family ruthlessly for the next few months. We had no peace. I recall when my oldest daughter was around four years of age and was scared, I told her that there was no need to be scared because our home was the safest place on earth and nothing could bother her here. I had let her down. What seemed like our sanctuary was now our torture chamber. Guilt again was rearing its taunting head. This was my entire fault. I brought this here. "God, are you there? Why aren't you helping us?" Linda and Mike continued to check on us regularly and gave me support that I needed, they even traveled to Louisiana and visited the old home place. I could tell that they both were unnerved when they departed. Later, Linda admitted that they both felt the evil presence that was there.

Chapter 11

TORMENT. UP UNTIL THAT POINT, I can honestly say that I had never experienced true torment. The agony felt like I was physically being pulled apart, but the events that followed were worse than agony. It was the cliché "hell on earth", or should I say, it was hell inside our home. It was literally constant chaos and negativity among us. The girls were at each other's throats, Jamie and I could merely breathe, and it would annoy the other. The tension in the air was so thick that it clung to my skin as I walked through it.

Nighttime came again with much dread. The spirits, who had once disguised themselves in a cloak of dark haze, were manifesting clearly before my eyes. They were clearly evoking my fear, and I had recently learned why: to gain strength. More than one pastor would advise me to show no fear. My feelings about demons were similar to the way I feel about snakes. If I see them from a distance, I can calmly face the situation. However, if I don't see it until I'm right by it, my fight or flight system overloads with fear. When I would be driving at night, on many occasions, a face would appear directly behind me in the rear view mirror; when putting on makeup in front of a mirror, a face would appear, snarling and showing its razor teeth. Now these folks who told me to show no fear would probably be checking their underwear for stains.

Bedtime was a nightmare. I would lie down with the girls at night until they all were asleep. They fought over who slept by me; so, usually, the two older girls slept on each side of me and Joanie would lie on top of me. The faces that hovered in the corners of the rooms were bad enough, but sometimes we saw nothing more than a black cloud moving toward us on the bed. I would tell it to stop in the name of Jesus, but it would plow through us. We retreated to my mother-in-law's home several nights, just to discover that something followed us wherever we went. One night at my mother-in-law's, the girls and I were sleeping in the living room. My oldest daughter slept in a sleeping bag on the floor, the baby slept in the recliner, while my middle daughter slept on the opposite end of the couch. I awoke around 3:30 AM to find the room hazy with thick black fog. My God, I thought, we can't have peace anywhere. I had been taking pictures around our house, but thus far they were blurry, dark, and hard to see. I did have a couple of videos of the black fog slowly creeping out of a closet, and the black fog swirling like a twister from behind the bed. I turned on my cell to video the room. First I videoed without the camera light being on, as the TV and lamp lit the room well enough. Then, I turned camera light on and filmed the entire room again, adding a bit of light into this darkness of ours. It was three days later that I watched the video on my cell. I couldn't believe my eyes. I showed it to my sister-in-law, LaJune, to validate what I saw. She, too, saw what I had seen. The atmosphere was literally spinning; it made the video appear to be blurry, but it was clear there was something sinister in the room. From the light of the TV, a dark figure was crouched over my child who was sleeping on the floor. It's not clear exactly what it was doing. There was a tall black silhouette of a man standing in front of the window. That could all be explained by a skeptic as merely shadows in a dark room, but the end of the clip that I filmed just three feet away was very clear. There was a side view of a demonic head and directly in front of the head was an apparition of a dog standing on its hind legs with front leg propped on the couch. The huge face was evil; it had small, recessed eyes with a strong nose and teeth that appeared to be long and razor sharp. I kept hearing a strange noise; so, I turned up the volume. Smacking and licking noises? What? Then I saw the source. My six year old was asleep between the dog and the disturbing face. When I enlarged the image, there was something red flicking in and out from between those piranha teeth. That thing, that creature, that demon, was licking my child! I realized this was even more evil than I imagined, even during our sleep. I started keeping myself awake; I only allowed myself the occasional catnap.

I was also concerned about spirits infiltrating my mother-in-law's home. The demons were a disease which was rapidly spreading throughout my life, and while I had the diagnosis, I failed to see a clear prognosis of this situation. I learned the spreading of this demon phenomenon is referenced as demonic transference. Jamie's younger brother lived there with his wife and young son. I didn't want anyone to have to go through the hell we were suffering, not even my worst enemy. Before this moment, this would have been something I would have jokingly wished upon an enemy of mine; now, with this experience of mine, I had learned a valuable lesson about humanity and how we should treat one another. No longer was I a self-centered, judgemental, heart of a person; I was softening to the pains of others. I was partially broken and didn't realize that more brokenness was to come. I was falling and failing as a Christian. I was so headstrong, determined to do things my way, to be in control. I'm sure God was thinking, poor child; she's going to have to learn the hard way. I did, however, see the world in a new light. I literally had love for other's overflowing from my heart.

I used to despise and loathe my sister-in-law, LaJune, because she had an addiction to narcotics after surviving a near fatal car accident. I thought she was lazy; she was a poor excuse of a human being. She had never personally inflicted harm on me; I had never offered a Christian hand or heart to her or her suffering. I judged her without cause. I judged a lot of people without cause. I was selfish, hard-hearted and very judgmental to certain types of people. I was a do-gooder, holier-than-thou, little miss perfect, and it took a catastrophic life event to adjust my attitude. I had to stumble and fall into sin to be humbled. Sin I proudly boasted I would NEVER commit. My sister-in-law became a close friend who not only would listen when I needed an ear, but she also wasn't too afraid to stay inside my home. She even witnessed several things that happened there and stood by me even though it scared her. I admired her for not only overcoming her addiction, but for her willingness to forgive me and then stand by me. One night LaJune and I were returning from last minute Christmas shopping and I could feel and smell that there was something in the vehicle with us. Not wanting to add fuel to the fire at home by bringing anything new home, I slowly pulled off of the dark deserted rural highway.

"What are you doing?" LaJune asked.

I calmly replied that I didn't want to freak her out, but we were not alone and that I intended to stop in order to pray. I had prayed before while driving and the fog-like darkness would encircle my head, nearly causing me to wreck. I leaned over and turned the radio down that was blaring holiday music and just as I released the knob, a deep growl came from the direction of the dash. I jerked my hand back and shrieked like I had touched fire. I saw a mass of black hovering just two or three feet away, near the windshield. I fumbled with my cell, well, because I had to try to document or break a leg trying. When I turned the phone towards the mass, a loud growl arose from my cell, causing it to vibrate simultaneously and I released it instantly, staring in disbelief as it bounced off the seat and onto floor. LaJune said, "What the heck?"

We stared at each other with wide eyes, thankful that we were in the company of one another when this incident happened. I began to pray earnestly, begging God to pluck this growling thing out of my vehicle. It remained, even after I dropped her off, it was after me. I drove up to our home and just sat behind the wheel praying loudly. I refused to go inside and have something new, something that growled viciously, attached to me. My kids deserved peace.

I continued praying, begging for God to intercede. I cried out that I was at the end of my rope, that I couldn't take much more. I should not have uttered that last statement. My mouth would, inevitably, get me in trouble.

Chapter 12

A CO-WORKER WHO KNEW THE REALITY of demonic spirits referred me to her pastor. Pastor Duke came twice and blessed house. Then he told me about a lady in his congregation who was involved in the deliverance ministry. I went to church that following Sunday. I went to the altar for prayer. Pastor Duke asked all prayer warriors to lay hands on me. I recall him telling the church that this was serious, that it involved demonic forces. After praying for me, one lady asked me how I felt, and I said good, but that was nothing more than a lie. I felt like a turd that had just been smeared onto freshly shampooed carpet. I met with the deliverance lady right after the service ended. We sat at a table as I solemnly answered all of her questions. Was I molested as a child? Yes, but that had been put behind me, I assured her. I had forgiven my molester and moved on from that bad memory. She asked me to repeat a prayer after her and I did, but it wasn't sincere because I was already annoyed by her lackadaisical attitude. Before I knew it, she was towering above me as I sat in the chair. She was an intimidating woman because she was several inches taller than me, and I was right at six feet tall. She leaned toward me as she yelled loudly in my right ear. "Line up in rank and order and come out of her now," she screamed more than once. What's she talking about, I wondered. This is nuts, I thought to myself, surely she doesn't think I'm possessed. Then she snapped her fingers in front of my face and yelled, "Come out from behind her eyes demon!!" What? I looked at her and said, "Lady I'm not possessed."

She slapped the back of my head with her Bible and yelled, "Shut up, demon!!" I was not only shocked at this but very annoyed, insulted and angry. I repeated sternly, "I'm not possessed, I told you." Again, I was hit in the back of the head with the Bible.

"Demon, don't speak unless I tell you too," she yelled directly into my ear again.

This was ridiculous. I assured her I was okay as I got to my feet and stepped out of arms' reach from this woman. She was breathing heavily and her eyes were wide. I told her I had to go and she told me that I needed deliverance, and she was going to get me some material to read. She wrote her name and number on a sheet of paper and gave it to me. I took it, thanked her for her time and threw the paper in the garbage on my way out of the door. Of all the absurd situations I had endured trying to get out of the mess I had brought upon myself, this one took the cake. I know it took a couple days to get over being insulted. Needless to say, I never contacted her again. I laugh when I recall that scene; I wish I could have been a fly on the wall.

Chapter 13

MEANWHILE, I HEARD A SPIRITUAL WARFARE REVIVAL
was being held in a neighboring town. I was given the pastor's number; so, I gave
him a brief rundown of the situation, and he scheduled a time to meet privately
with him and his wife. I was relieved that Jamie went with me and hopefully I
wouldn't get assaulted by God's word. We sat facing them in a cozy little church
office. He asked a lot of questions, similar to the questions I had been asked
before, only he prodded deeper into my emotions. Apparently, I still held resentment towards my mother for the way I felt she handled the whole molestation
issue when it was revealed. I felt like an outcast, as if I had done something wrong,
and I felt like my mother was sympathizing with him. I am sure she handled it to
the best way she knew how, trying to maintain peace. When the proverbial dust
settled, not one word was ever mentioned about it again, because molestation
and demons were classed together, or perhaps I should say, both topics caused
the same nervous reaction because both were considered taboo. Believing in such
horrid notions causes most to bury their heads in the sand. But, as easy as it is
to ignore the atrocities of life, in the end, when the heads are removed from the
sand, the problem is still present, and they are left with grit in their eyes. In other
words, pretending there is not a problem does nothing but prolong the situation.

The minister and his wife sat looking at me. He kept encouraging me to talk
about the painful events in my past. I choked back bitter tears. I heard him tell me

to pray out loud, asking God to forgive my unforgiveness. My eyes were closed, when I heard a strange, deep and raspy voice talking. I tried to open my eyes, but I felt like my entire body was tied up. I felt like a puppet. I heard him ask Jamie if he had ever heard me talk like that before; he said no. Then he told Jamie to hold me still in my chair. I heard the man call my name; so, I looked up, and he asked if I heard what just happened. I nodded yes. He asked me what I thought. I told him that either I was not a Christian, or I had multiple personalities. He laughed and replied that neither was true. He explained that contrary to what most churched people believed, Christians can have a demon. This was news to me because I was totally ignorant in regards to demons and spiritual warfare. I didn't know the difference between possession, oppression or demonization. I had a lot to learn. He explained a Christian can have a demon and be influenced by it, much like a Christian who has sin such as alcoholism or pornography. The more that particular sin in indulged in, the more power and control it has over the Christian's thoughts and life. He said possession refers to ownership and a demon cannot own a blood bought believer, however, they can keep them in bondage. Demons can invade the body, but not the spirit of the person. Again, he commanded the spirit within me to come to the surface. Again, I could hear another voice talking, but my mouth was moving in synchronization with the voice. The spirit was commanded out, and this time I leaned forward and exhaled and exhaled until I felt like my insides were turned inside out. I was breathing heavily and felt so tired. Despite the way I felt, the minister pressed further. He asked if there were any more demons inside of me. I nodded yes, but I wasn't sure. He asked for a name. The voice said, Failure. The more information that came out, the angrier the demon got. Jamie said it was a struggle to physically keep me in the chair. The spirit divulged that failure was present because of my father and my inability to please him. I had always felt that if I were perfect enough or worked hard enough, I would gain his approval. The minister told Jamie that my father was the stronghold. Stronghold? What does that mean? He explained that a stronghold is a thought or action or influential person who controls our minds or our way of thinking/reasoning. Examples of strongholds can include: pornography, addictions, depression, murder, money, power, hatred, jealousy, adultery, etc. These can be controlled by demonic forces, which is how the enemy uses these tactics -- he knows our weaknesses. When that sronghold is identified, confessed and broken, then and only then can a person be truly delivered, unshackled, and set free. Again, all sins and addictions are not caused by a demonic spirit. Sometimes it is the person's choice and free will.

When I realized where I was, I wondered why I was on my knees in the floor. The minister asked me how I felt. I felt like a burden was lifted, but I still did not feel free. I didn't mention the latter feeling of still being bound by something that I couldn't even describe.

We walked away that day with mixed emotions, but he had referred us to a local pastor who was training in the deliverance ministry. I met with this man one Wednesday afternoon in a nearby town. Again, I was met with redundant questions. He gathered my hurt that I was feeling due to my parents' lack of belief. He thought surely if I let this go that the torment would stop. He also quizzed me repeatedly as to whether or not I had ever partaken in any form of witchcraft or voodoo. No, no Ouija board, no séances, nothing, I stated. He made the comment more than once that due to the severity and nature of the demonic attack we were experiencing, there must be something dark, something of a satanic nature in my past. NO! I repeatedly said. But the thought gnawed at my soul like a satiated dog, chewing on a bone for mere pleasure.

Back at home, my family continued to be knee deep in hell. Sitting in front of my computer, which was located in the dining room, I decided I was going to research spiritual warfare tactics. I was eating scrambled eggs, attempting to acquire some form of nourishment. I looked like I had anorexia, but mine was not due to perceiving myself overweight. I was just distracted by utter chaos at mealtime, and by the time that I could eat in peace, my appetite was gone. It took only a few bites to make me feel full or nauseous. That morning, the bright sunshine was streaming in like it was determined to lighten my foreboding mood. Shadows began to streak behind me causing shadows to flicker in the room. I told myself it was only birds flying outside the window, but had that been the case, then the bird population had multiplied two fold overnight. Something did not like me searching for knowledge in ways to defeat and overcome demonic oppression. To my left, on the eggshell white wall, bright bluish orange colored light appeared long enough to get my attention. It was a glowing ball of light that seemed to explode and disperse. As my eyes remained fixed on the wall, my vision blurred, and then my vision re-focused. The wall appeared 3-D as it bulged like liquid were moving in it. Letters that were about three to four inches tall were forming before my eyes and protruded out of the wall. I rubbed my eyes and shook my head as if to sling whatever was causing this illusion out of my eyes. Still there. It wasn't English, and I had no idea what it meant, but it unnerved me because it was to say the least, inconceivable. I was in such a state of shock that by the time I thought to grab the camera, the letters retreated into the wall as if a powerful vacuum sucked them out of existence. I felt like I was losing my ever-loving mind. That could not have really happened! Yet I knew it had, and it was only the start of this evil force's tactics to torment my mind. I called one of the ladies from the paranormal group, she told me to take a picture. Well, I tried, I explained.

Again, I met with the minister from a nearby town. I was annoyed and tiring of being asked the same questions. No, I have not ever been involved in the occult. No, I have never dabbled in dark magic. Have I ever been involved with anything satanic? Rituals? Black magic? No, no and what? Black? My mind was whirling, spinning out of control as my subconscious battled with the notion of reality. My God, No! No, No, No! I kept shaking my bowed head as tears built up against a dam that I tried to hold together.

"What did you do?" I heard his voice coming from what sounded like a barrel and it echoed in my mind.

"I remember," I tried to say, but was not clear through my clenched teeth. My jaw was shut so forcefully, I thought my teeth might shatter. My whole body was rigid as I battled with my mind, my memories that I had so meticulously buried within the very core of my being.

"What happened, Joy, talk to me. Joy!" No, I can't. No I won't. Leave this where it is, Joy, I said to myself.

But I heard myself saying, "Honduras, a black room." Then my willpower overcame that thought, and I looked up and said, "No, I can't recall anything."

He knew I was hiding something. I was good at it, too. Pretend all is well and life will be wonderful, at least in the public's eyes. He asked if he could come to my house for a meeting with my husband and me. No, my mind told me, but I nodded yes.

Chapter 14

BACK HOME, I CALLED ANGELA. I could hear doubt in her voice.
Then I called the pastor's wife from our Baptist church. She asked how well I
knew this preacher. She insinuated that perhaps they were somehow planting
these satanic ideas in my mind for some other purpose. Then came the question
that was a turning point and not for the better. She asked if I had recently had a
CAT scan of my brain. I informed her that yes, as a matter of fact I had an MRI
just four months earlier. I quickly ended the conversation, and I had a temper
tantrum unlike any before. I slammed the phone on the hardwood floor and
cursed like an angry sailor. I just happened to glance up towards the bathroom
and saw a full body apparition slowly moving toward me. I wasn't scared; I was
furious. "You son of a bi***! Why don't you and your friends pack your demon
a**es and leave! None of you are welcome here! Y'all have made me look like a
d*** lunatic, and I'm sick of y'all scaring my girls." I walked right up to the apparition and looked up at its eyes and sternly raised my voice again. "I know you
hear me, you piece of demon sh**t! Get out!" The apparition started swirling
from the floor up, causing the human- shaped figure to dissipate into a cloudy
mass of black smoke. I stepped back and although it made no noise, it whooshed
right through my chest, causing me to stagger backwards. I felt nothing when
it passed through me other than a prickly, static sensation. I would soon learn

that each time these entities made physical contact they gained strength from my body, which in turn was making me progressively weaker and stricken with unusual health issues for my age.

Every outburst of anger from me or Jamie, or quarreling among the girls or any fear shown at all was demon food. I am ashamed to say it took a long time to figure this out. Furthermore, even after we gained that knowledge, it was so hard not to be angry or scared, given what was occurring. The minister who had been working with me to get to the root of the problem planned to come to our house. I invited a couple from our former church to be there with us for support, Brad and Pam. Deep down, I knew the flood gates of my soul were about to open, I felt the pressure building. That evening our guests and I sat in our living room making small talk. The couple who joined us asked the minister many questions regarding demons and spiritual warfare. The preacher sat on the couch, and I sat in the rocking chair a few feet in front of him. He began by asking me to close my eyes. Then he took my thoughts back in time and asked specific questions to lure my innermost thoughts to the surface. He did not "hypnotize" me by any means, just made me clear my mind and focus on past events. No! My mind resisted. I did not want to remember any painful events. Just let sleeping dogs lie, as my grandmother used to say. No sense in bringing up things from the past that you can't change. Life goes on, don't go back and relive it. That is what I was telling myself, but I could hear my voice defying my wishes. Yes, I remember a black room as I choked back tears. Honduras. Mission trip. My God. No! But I spoke anyway.

I stopped as we approached the small home, made of mud that was tucked into lush, green overgrowth on the mountain side. I paused to take a picture and flashed a smile at Gibby, one of the translators who was assigned to the medical mission team that I was with. I was thrilled he offered to walk through the remote village with me so I could get a more personal perspective of the primitive lifestyle of the Honduran people. We had visited two homes already, and I was in awe of how content and happy the people appeared to be, despite their circumstances. Gibby knocked on the door and stepped behind me as a short man with graying hair opened the door. He was wearing brown pants that were rolled up above his ankles and was not wearing a shirt. As I looked past him into the house, my body instinctively stiffened because I knew this old country girl was in big trouble. I took two steps backward and bumped into Gibby, who placed a firm hand in the small of my back, nudging me forward. I said that I wanted to go back to the camp. No, he told me, the men in the room were his friends, and they just wanted to talk with me for a little while. Then, he gave me one big shove into the house and closed the door, just as the deepest recesses of my mind began to close its own door in order to survive this nightmare.

The walls were as black as my soul felt in my subconscious mind that was spiraling into a secret place of silent seclusion. There was no furniture in the one room, dirt floor shack. There was a large circle scratched into the dirt in the center of the room. The graying Honduran man, along with five other younger men dressed in the same fashion, approached me. They were all smiling and talking among themselves in Spanish. My clothes and shoes were removed as I struggled with every ounce of strength I could muster. I ended up on my back in the middle of the circle as a rope was tied to each wrist and ankle. Four of the men each held a rope as they began to pull the rope tightly enough to cause me to look like human "X". My tears dripped off the side of my face and landed in the thirsty dirt. I begged Gibby to help me, but he sternly told me to shut up as he backed into the shadows of the wall. The graying man stood at my feet and stared down at me with a maniacal smile. The fifth man placed white candles around the circle and lit them, then quickly retrieved a tray from the shadowy floor. The graying man took a stick from the tray, along with a large cup. The stick, which was about two feet long, looked similar to a sawed off broom handle. The graying man began to chant, and the others followed suit. He dipped the stick into the cup and then flicked it towards me. I felt something wet splatter me from head to toe. The liquid splattered my lips, and I tasted salty blood. He continued chanting as he knelt between my spread legs. I was having my period at the time, and the man grabbed my tampon string and yanked it out. He dipped the stick into the blood-filled cup and swiftly shoved it into my vagina. The pain seared through my pelvis, and I screamed a high pitched sound that pierced my own ears. Then, he dipped the stick in blood again and shoved it into my rectum. I had never felt such intense pain before. My mind started to shut down with each violent push and pull of the stick. I kept repeating the same thing over in my mind: This Is Not REAL!!! This CANNOT be happening on a mission trip.

God would Not ALLOW this to happen to a Christian. This is not real; it's just a bad, bad nightmare.

I had been so naive and ignorant of the reality of evil. I thought satanic worship only existed in horror movies. I really thought I was going to die in that little house that day. In order to push that thought aside, I began thinking about family and friends back home. I could almost hear my cynical father telling me that he knew I didn't have any business going over to that country to begin with, so "it's all your fault." I remember the day I was to be baptized; my father told me not to depend on "religion" to get me through life. He told me that religion was for weak people, who couldn't stand on their own two feet. I have come to realize that his statement was partially true because from the day I accepted Christ as my Lord and Savior, I have yet to stand on my own spiritual feet. He carried me the entire time because I never even put a toe on the ground. Jesus carried me the entire time. The pain jolted my mind back to the nightmare I was living. Gibby was standing over me, naked from the waist down. As I felt the weight of his body on top of me, I cried out, "God, please! No! Then Gibby yelled out in Spanish, then English, "We found our virgin!" The six men cheered and yelled out joyously, as if their team had scored a touchdown.

Music had always had a way of comforting me. It seemed as if there was a song for each situation in life and singing about it helped to release tension. The music in my mind was Enigma's "Return to Innocence;" it was soothing. My thoughts then drifted to my boyfriend back home. I knew he was the "one" I would live the rest of my life with. He and I grew up together. He even told me in Kindergarten that he was going to marry me. I seriously doubted that statement at the time, but it made me feel special. I even went to the senior prom with him but only as a friend. Years later, when his fiancé was unfaithful, and they broke up, I felt sorry for Jamie. So, therefore, when he asked me out, I reluctantly agreed. I was reluctant because I was already feeling God calling me into the foreign mission field. I didn't want to get distracted because I didn't want to let God down. Jamie and I dated six months before I even held his hand and nearly another six months before I kissed him. I remember how ironic it was that my strict, over-protective father told me that I needed to hug him, kiss him, or do something because if he were Jamie, he would have dumped me a long time ago. I wanted to avoid intimacy; I wanted to save my purity. After revealing the rape, a pastor explained that even though my virginity was taken against my will, I still maintained my spiritual virginity. That really did not ease my mind.

I truly fell in love with Jamie while watching Disney's *The Hunchback of Notre Dame* in the theater. Asking him to watch that movie was a test. I figured he would be miserable and would be unable to hide his misery. Near the middle of the movie; however, I heard him laughing, really laughing; so, I turned and looked up at him. He was genuinely enjoying the movie. He was a child at heart, too. I had found my soul mate.

My mind drifted back to the present. Gibby got up, and I felt a drop of his sweat burn my chest. More chanting ensued with great climactic enthusiasm. Each man walked past me, dipped their thumbs in blood and pressed their bloody thumb onto my forehead. I was allowed to sit up, and one of the men threw a dirty towel in my face and sat a small bucket of water in front of me. He said something in Spanish, but Gibby nodded at him, and then looked at me and told me to clean up and get dressed. I remember gagging when I wiped that putrid rag across my bloody face. I was trembling all over, from fear and from pain. The pain in my pelvic and rectal area was excruciating. It felt as if there was a knife inside of me. Apparently, I was taking too long because Gibby jerked the rag from my hand and scrubbed any exposed skin that had blood on it. Then he dumped the water from the bucket in my lap. There was a lot of blood still trickling from either my rectum or vagina; I wasn't sure which. The dirt had blood mixed in it everywhere, and flies were starting to take notice. I stood up with wobbly legs and had to bend over at the waist and hold my stomach due to severe cramping. I fumbled with my clothes, trying my best to move quickly. Gibby stood there tapping his foot and telling me to hurry up. As we walked out the door, he draped something around my shoulders. We walked back to camp in total silence. In fact, I didn't even speak or make eye contact with him the remainder of the trip; my mind was still downloading the event into a neat little folder to be filed away in my brain. Gibby was not the only one I avoided the following days in Central America. I avoided God too.

Chapter 15

AFTER TEARFULLY AND PAINFULLY RECOUNTING to the best of my ability the horrific details, I opened my eyes to see my husband's shocked, yet understanding look. No doubt, knowing what I had been through made some of my odd behavior make total sense, especially in regards to our intimate relationship. Pam clarified my virginity, asking whether or not I was penetrated when molested as a child. I nodded no. Then came the hard part; the minister asked me to forgive the men who had destroyed my faith, destroyed my purity and contaminated my little, simple life with demonic forces. He made me realize that not only had I been dragging generational spirits through life, but I had been contaminated through that occultist ritual, explaining that when each man pressed a bloody thumb print on my forehead, it was transferring demonic spirits to me, not to mention how the sodomy and rape introduced them into me as well. He explained that it didn't matter whether I was a child of God or not. I was demonized. That is why, he explained, I was unaware of why certain events occurred in my life: unusual health problems, miscarriages, marital problems, and doubts about God and religion. But I've been told by many pastors that Christians cannot be possessed, that evil cannot be in the presence of the Holy Spirit and it leaves most Christians vulnerable and defenseless to demonic attacks. A lot of times, demons can enter into a person before they become a

Christian. Therefore, continuing to control or influence the physical body. I began studiously reading scripture to confirm my suspicions that the enemy has crept through back door of our organized religion and infiltrated and placed blindfolds upon church goers. Given what I experienced, I think it's just ridiculous to sit and argue and speculate as to whether a person is saved or lost when there is a human being needing deliverance. It is obvious that the Spiritual war wages all around us, and Satan is the ringleader. He constantly feeds the world false information about himself and his plans. Many people, including Christians, dismiss his existence, even though the Bible makes clear reference to him. This denial makes his mission to destroy Christians even easier, because they don't expect his tactics. The Bible provides the intelligence for the Christian to understand just how Satan operates, so his strategies and tactics will not take us in. We need to understand, we are at war and under attack. Understanding who our enemy is and how he operates allows us to prepare for the attack, putting us on the offensive, rather the defensive.

I tried to say that I forgave my attacker; that was hard. The preacher asked me to call out to Jesus for help. "J-J-J...." I couldn't make the name roll off my tongue.

The remainder of events was told to me by my husband because I have no memory of what transpired over the next thirty minutes. A deep male voice came from my mouth. No! The minister spoke to this voice, and it became very angry. The voice refused to say Jesus. The voice was cocky and arrogant. The voice cursed the preacher. The preacher commanded the demon to reveal his name. The voice spoke another language, repeating the same phrase repeatedly. The voice screamed in anguish as my body contorted and tried to get out of the rocking chair. It took four people to keep my frail body in the chair. The spirit would not relent and say Jesus, but it finally spoke a name. The name it voiced, I refuse to even type. I refused to allow this demon to get any credit or be praised by any satanic worshiper for a job well done.

When "Joy" was back in control, I was just shocked, embarrassed, and horrified at what had just happened. Everyone was Googling the words that had been spoken through me, trying to decipher what was said and in what language. What was spoken was not clear, but it mentioned "the comatose years." Since I came back from that fateful mission trip, my life had been a blur; a blur in regards to everything. I had been going through the motions of life, not truly living. The language was Portuguese. I had never been taught, formally or informally, any other language besides Southern English.

Again, these events made me feel "crazy" and embarrassed. And again, I questioned my sanity and God. But the night was not over. The preacher asked me to identify the number of spirits I saw. The demonic spirits were all different. They each looked different. Some had human characteristics; some looked like pictures of the devil portrayed in books or in horror movies. These spirits had migrated to the dining room, adjacent to where we sat. The preacher asked me if I had anything from Honduras in my home. Yes, I had pictures, a necklace, carved wooden statues that I could remember. He asked me to go find these objects. My husband and I dug frantically through closets, jewelry boxes, and through boxes in the attic. I showed them a picture of the translator. Jamie stared at his image hard, with anger in his eyes. We all walked outside, and the pastor asked us all to pray out loud as we walked around the house. I could barely breathe, but didn't say a word about the intense resistance I was experiencing. As I walked along, listening to the others praying, I attempted to say a prayer out loud too. I was shoved from behind by unseen hands and landed face down in the grass; I could not move or call out for help. The pastor happened to glance at me lying there, and I was assisted to my feet. Brad spoke up and said he thought we needed to burn the objects from Honduras now, not wait. One last time I was drilled if I had been given jewelry or any gift by the translator. Oh my goodness, he did give me something. After the rape, when I was halfway cleaned and dressed, the translator draped a jacket across my shoulders. But I was so numb at this point, I couldn't think straight. I simply put it in the bottom of my suitcase, much like I put that evening's events in the bottom of my mind, tucked away safely so I could resume my existence of pretending life was perfect. I recall giving a moving testimony before my church, telling them what an awesome, moving experience the trip had been. I impressed myself at my ability to survive and pretend like I actually enjoyed surviving. These thoughts were in my mind as I reached into the back of my closet and pulled out the coat. It was multi-colored, handmade, stuffed with cotton. The old Dolly Parton song sang out in my mind as I took the coat outside. Everything was piled up in the driveway, a prayer was said and a fire started. It was then that the cows started mooing loudly, not just one, but many cows. Nearby dogs began barking, our Bassett Hound, who never made a sound, was sitting in the grass beside us howling continuously. As the fire engulfed those things, I was choking, smothered, and was brought to my hands and knees. I coughed and exhaled as I felt something release from deep inside me. I got back on my feet and smiled because I did feel better. We all sang *Amazing Grace* as we watched part of my past disappearing within the flames. The preacher asked if we could walk around the house once more and make sure I didn't see anything. Well, I did. The pastor told Jamie, that as the spiritual leader of the house, he had to take authority and evict the remaining trespassers. I would point to where they were hovering, and Jamie would yell and rebuke them. Sometimes, he would reach out as if physically grabbing them and squeezing them until they disappeared. Everyone was so elated and celebrating a victory. I was smiling too, but still I felt burdened. What was wrong with me? Why is this going on and on? Is God punishing me? Again, I had to put on my happy face and tell the world all was well. But inside my home, the enemy was getting ready for another attack. Something was determined to kill me or drive me insane.

Chapter 16

I WAS ON A MISSION. I WAS STALKING those boogers and taking pictures and videos in an effort to expose their reality. Some pastors said to gather evidence and proof, while some said to ignore them because capturing their image gave them more strength. I think there was some truth in both suggestions. I know they did not like me taking pictures; it made them hiss and snarl. I also know that if I ignored them, they would really get ballsy and more dramatic with their antics. One thing that was done to force me to acknowledge them was to stomp and hiss at the girls when they came through doorways. They would not go to their bedrooms alone to change clothes, get a toy, or go to the bathroom alone. The fact that my kids were basically prisoners in their home infuriated me. Two years of their childhood was shrouded in fear, isolation, embarrassment, confusion, and anger. They missed out on having birthday parties and sleep overs. They were ruthlessly teased at school. If not directed at them, they would be told that their mom was crazy or nuts. It was not only children partaking in the mockery; it was also ignorant adults. The girls even came home repeating things they had heard my parents say. I would have loved to allow anyone to walk in my shoes just one day and night to see if they could have handled the pressure.

I had followed the well-meaning advice of many. I had Bibles open to the pages with the red letters of Christ in every room; gospel music blaring from the televisions and radios; the demons were capable of turning the music off, so apparently it was offensive. I had blessed prayer cloths in every pillow slip, crosses around our necks, and crucifixes in each room. What it boiled down to was that those were all just religious things. I also had been given books with prayers to defeat demons and break curses. Those were just words. What made all that effective was the faith behind them. My faith at that point was severely handicapped. I was praying, God was listening, but I didn't know it. I felt like I must have deserved this madness. Once again, I turned outside the church for help. I was scrolling through the normal lives of others on Facebook one night and noticed a cousin was discussing her recent exploration of a cemetery and was discussing the pictures she had taken. I jokingly responded to her that if she wanted to see some real boogers, to call me. Well, she did.

After telling her what was happening, Liz said, "My God! Girl, those ain't no regular ghosts, you got yourself some demons!"

She said she knew some guys who could help. The very next day, The Paranormal Society of Ponchatoula called me. They came out quickly to see what they could do. The two guys climbed out of their trucks and walked up with their equipment in hand. Both of them were looking around, and I could tell by their expressions that they were sensitive to the paranormal. The tall dark-headed one was the founder of the group. Kenny asked a few questions, but he was a man of few words. His partner, Jereme, was blond and loved to talk. He had a look of grave concern in his eyes as he listened to my story. Also, I saw a sympathetic look of pity. Both seemed genuinely concerned for our safety. As they started getting their cameras out, they noticed the batteries were draining quickly and other equipment was malfunctioning. They knew it was not coincidence. They both felt the heavy pressure in the house and stated it was difficult to breathe for them as well. The older girls were playing quietly in the living room, and little Joanie was asleep in her bed. Kenny went into the room where Joanie slept to try to film the room that had the most activity. Jereme was walking around the house alone. As I stood in the hallway outside of Joanie's room, I looked to my right through the bathroom and saw the apparition of the skinny man forming under the attic. What? Kenny asked. I stepped into the bedroom and repeated my description of what I saw in the hallway. I had just got the words out of my mouth when we heard Jereme tearing through the bathroom and literally jumping into the kitchen. He breathlessly said several curse words, and I could see that his face was completely drained of color. Now I had a look of concern for him. He explained that he just saw an f-ing full body apparition. He said as he walked through the bathroom, he glanced in the mirror and saw it standing in front the master bedroom door, and it was staring directly at him. As he described the tall man that towered somewhere near seven feet tall with long arms that went to right below the knees, he saw long fingers with long fingernails. He said the man was bald on top and had an unusually elongated face with a bushy beard. That confirmed my description exactly to Kenny. And, that validity felt as good as a warm blanket on a cold night. I waited in the living room with the kids as they filmed in Joanie's room. When they emerged, they told me they had caught some stuff. The baby had awakened during the recording and told them that the mean man was outside. They agreed to come back and do a full investigation. As the three of us walked outside into the peaceful, clear night, discussing their return, something in the air changed immediately. The wind went from nonexistent to gale force in a matter of seconds. When I say gale force, I mean patio chairs flipping over and blowing off the patio. Also, garbage can lids and other debris went flying by us. The unexplained wind was so loud that the investigators and I couldn't understand one another. They drove away, and when they turned onto the highway, the wind stopped just as quickly as it started. Kenny texted me back and said he just looked at satellite weather and no storm in the vicinity.

Back inside, Joanie had gotten up, and all three girls were standing in the kitchen; I could clearly see that something was wrong by the terrified, wide-eyed look they all held. My middle daughter, who preferred not to discuss the subject at all, was biting her fingernails. I asked them what happened, what was wrong?

The oldest said, "Mommy! They're after us!"

The middle daughter grabbed my leg in a frenzied panic and started crying. I asked her, what? She pointed and frantically said that the hunched-over man was coming. I knew which one she was referring to because I had seen him many times, and I was watching him shuffle closer, along with several more.

"What are they saying?" little Joanie asked.

It was then that I realized I was hearing them audibly. They were all talking at once, and it sounded more like a room full of murmurings. Some were hissing and snarling. I was nearly tackled as all three girls grabbed my legs and began crying in terror.

"Let's get outta here," I said, and I grabbed my keys off the counter and ushered my terrified girls to my SUV.

We drove a few miles, and I stopped and secured the girls in their seats. My fear urged me to call out to God, something I hadn't sincerely done in a couple of weeks. The girls sat quietly as I poured my heart out to God. I sincerely meant every pleading word. I drove forty-five minutes and checked into a motel room. Ahhh, this would be precious sleep, or so I thought. The girls bounced around happily, except for little Joanie. She was quiet as her eyes darted around the room. What's wrong? I questioned her. She twirled her nervous little fingers in her hair and looked at me with the eyes of a soldier who was about to enter into battle, knowing she must face the inevitable with bravery and show no fear.

"He wanted to come with us Mommy," I heard her reply.

What? Who? Which one? She would never say. But I soon knew. I heard him talking. It was the one with the filthy language. My God, there was no escape.

We returned home the next day. As we drove down the long gravel driveway, we were all silent. I believe we were all four having the same feeling of dread. Dreading what terror we would face next. These things were gaining strength, and their antics became more intense with each battle. The enemy was planting booby traps, and I was becoming entangled in every one. LaJune, her husband, and son stayed with us for two nights. I was so relieved, not because they offered protection, but because they were adults with whom I could simply hold a conversation.

However, the activity did not always lessen while they were there. One night Joanie was taking a bubble bath, when she yelled for me to come quickly. I burst into the already open doorway with LaJune trailing behind. Joanie was giggling in a silly manner and pointed at the shower door. "Look what he's doin', Mommy! "There, as clear as could be, amidst the smeared bubbles on the door was the evil face of the old bearded man. Some will try to disprove this, saying that it was happenstance, that the bubbles were like the clouds, merely appearing to take the shape of something, but we stood watching the face form like unseen hands were drawing it. I, of course, took a picture.

The PSP investigators returned. Jereme approached me and said in his southern drawl, "I'm gonna be honest with you, Joy, I really didn't wanna come back to this house; it scares the Hell outta me. I think some kind of portal has been opened here. Satan himself could possibly be coming in and out of your house." He had obviously spent a lot of time researching every avenue to help provide answers in an attempt to figure out how to bring our nightmare to an end. He sincerely cared and I often called him for advice and just to have someone to say, I understand.

I just nodded with a blank expression. I was being sucked under in the spinning drain of this nightmare. My mind was numb; my heart was beating to the rhythm of desperation. I didn't know how much more I could stand. But I was still holding onto "me" and "my." How stubborn could I be? My obstinate nature was killing me. I was trying to lean on God; yet I wouldn't take that load off my shoulders and leave it at the foot of the cross. Yes, I wanted redemption, but I wasn't willing to forgive myself; I deserved this punishment. I had to carry my own cross. God was still shaking His head. He kept holding out His hand to me, but I couldn't see it in the darkness.

The investigation went fine, nothing earth-shattering. The EVP session, which records voices that are inaudible to the human ear, recorded in the master bedroom, was just unsettling. Two entities acknowledged their presence; both were male. When asked their names, the question was answered with a question. "Who's this?" When I asked what they wanted with us, the response was "kids, kids, kids." Jereme asked, "Do you know you're a sick pervert?"

The reply was, "F***-you, f***-you, f***-you!"

When they drove away that night, I felt good that they had proof that something supernatural was occurring. But at the same time, well, I still didn't know how I could make my demons leave. Jereme later told me that he knew there was someone or something besides Joy looking through my eyes. He feared for my life.

Chapter 17

THE CALM BEFORE THE STORM HELD AN EERIE SILENCE,

a taunting silence. We even got some sleep. I think, sometimes, that God gave us two or three good weeks in between battles in order to rest and regroup. I cannot recall how many times we celebrated in vain. By this time, I had to return to work, as I had stretched my personal leave to four months. I was an RN at the local rural hospital. I loved my job, and I dearly loved my co-workers, who were like an extension of my family. I was not given my regular dayshift charge nurse position back due to the director's doubts about my stability. However, I enjoyed working the different day and night shifts because it kept some chaotic stability to my life. I loved a challenge, and I loved to stay busy. I thrived on the shifts where I had to juggle several challenging situations at once. I loved saving lives. I was a professional; yet I loved to add humor and lightheartedness to each day. Laughing with my co-workers was good therapy. I felt it would do some good to get back on a routine and take my mind off the past several months' events. It didn't take long, however, for hell to break loose again. I was in the dining room paying bills online at the computer desk. The back door was open to let the cool breeze inside. I heard a noise; I wasn't sure what it was, so I looked toward the back door. It was a bright sun-shining day, but sunlight could not infiltrate the utility room because it was nestled under the cover of the garage. But to my dismay, a shadow appeared on the wall, just inside the door. It took the shape of a tall man. The tall man, the bearded man, the mean man, or the boss. At some point, we had called him many names. The right side of the man was clear, including the long beard. I couldn't look away. The shadow lifted his hands as if he were scooping up sand. Then the apparition bent his head forward and blew in his cupped hands. To my utter disbelief, something was literally flying out of his hands. It was dark gray masses that were spinning like little tornados. They were whirling all over the house. I couldn't move or speak and didn't even pray within my mind. When he was finished, his shadowy figure changed into a large dark orb and streaked towards the back of the house. I leaned forward in the computer chair propping up with my elbows on my thighs. I cried. I sobbed. Surely this is not real. God, if you're there, please help me keep what little sanity I have left. We didn't tell anyone. It was very embarrassing to me that we would think it was gone, tell everyone, only to have to deal with it again. So I would pretend everything was fine. I kept nodding off at work when I had to sit still at the computer. If I stayed on my feet and stayed busy, I was fine. But lack of sleep was wearing me down fast. I realized I couldn't work under these circumstances. I had no choice but to resign. Walking away from the job I loved, the career I loved was heartbreaking. My world was spiraling toward the proverbial drain. Again, I thought to myself that it couldn't get much worse. How could I forget so quickly that I should not have that thought?

At home, Joanie was acting out aggressively, using foul language and laughing about it. She would look over my shoulder at something and laugh. During prayer time or during a meal and especially at bedtime something was causing a ruckus that I couldn't see. Joanie would often beg me not to read the Bible; she said it made them angry and they scared her by making mean faces. The girls all recounted that one of the demons always talked over me as I prayed beside them on the floor and they couldn't hear what I was saying to God. Bath time was the worst, though, because a naked apparition would appear on the back wall of the shower. It had an exaggerated sized penis and it would hold it and swing it from side to side. The girls would hastily wash and get out. I was determined to make these things leave on my own, just as some pastors' suggested. I was alone the next morning, so I grabbed my Bible and opened the back door to let the spirits out. I stood in the middle of the kitchen reading the Bible out loud. That always made them angry. Sure enough the tornado demons, as my middle daughter called them, surfaced in the back hallway that could be seen through the central bathroom. Some drifted down from the attic, some from my bedroom and most of them would come from within the walls, in which they would bulge out as if the sheetrock was comprised of a stretchy rubber. I continued reading verses that clearly made them angry. One of the main entities formed in the back hallway. It was smiling, not in a friendly way. It was mocking my efforts. It threw its head back with laughter. This particular spirit had a human torso, but its legs ended in hooves. It had a reptilian looking head. Its skin was green. It had a flat head, no hair, and odd shaped ears. Funny thing about it that I still don't understand is how can you hear the clicking of hooves on the floor when something that is not of this world is walking? As I read scripture and stood in the kitchen commanding them to leave in the name of Jesus, one spirit at a time came through the bathroom, into the kitchen and out the back door. It was a steady stream of white to black blurry masses. Many of them had faces and each one looked differently. I thought to myself that if lost folks, not to mention straying Christians, could see half of these things, they would repent quickly. Some looked like human faces, some like dogs, some like bulls, and some looked purely demonic with sharp teeth, fangs and horns. Some were just floating faces, others were full body figures. I felt good that they were obeying my command to leave, but there was one problem: they were passing through my body, and I was quickly feeling drained, sluggish, and dizzy. I refused to stop, but I become so weak that I got down on my knees and continued telling them to keep coming and leave my house. My voice was weakening; my words were becoming jumbled, and my mind was going dim. I could hear my voice, but it sounded like it was coming from deep within a room that echoed. I slumped to the floor and slept there for two hours. I was so weak; I could barely stand on my trembling legs. I called Angela to tell her what had happened. I had to stop; I had become too weak to continue. I couldn't do it. She asked me to listen to what I had just said; I wasn't sure what she meant.

"Who was casting them out, who became weak?" she replied.

"I did," I told her. What about The Lord, what part did He play? Okay, I got it now. I cannot do anything. I am weak, but He is strong. Angela always knew how to suggest things to try to keep me focused.

The harder I tried to rebuke the demons, like everyone suggested since they were my demons, the more intense the attacks became. I was extremely concerned with my two-year-olds behavior changes. The vulgar words and the inappropriate behavior continued, and I couldn't understand why one minute she was interacting with something as if it were her friend and terrified the next minute.

Chapter 18

IT WAS CONFIRMED BY PROFESSIONALS that there was some form of an evil presence in our home and that one in particular loved the two words "f*** you," which just so happened to be the choice word that two of my children had begun using. This was not a coincidence, I thought, or did I feed this into their little minds and corrupt their emotional well-being because my Parkinson's medication caused my mind to hallucinate? Or did I have a nervous breakdown and didn't exhibit any symptoms publicly? Did I stay awake day and night trying to stage videos and fake pictures? I asked the questions that I knew were being asked around me by people whom I once trusted and depended on; yet, I knew all of the answers to those questions. I was not the one responsible for these actions. I did call my friends, my family, my pastor to listen to me as I attempted to make sense of this, and what was occurring did scare them, and I knew as much as they wanted to and tried to, they didn't understand. My mind was racing with thoughts of how to handle this and how my family and I were going to survive. I had legitimate concerns. I was under tremendous stress. I became extremely sleep deprived. I sat and wondered how many of the naysayers would have survived even this far?

Would any of them have stayed in their seat if a male voice suddenly asked, "Hey, hey! What are you doing?" right behind their ear? Or would they have left running when a demonic spirit materialized behind them as they were about to leave and said, "Hey, hey! Where are you going?"

I was tempted to really mess with the minds of the ones who thought I had lost my marbles. It intrigued me that some people were frightened to even associate with me or come within a few feet of me. I laugh to myself at the childish notions I would entertain, but I would never do, well, because I was sane. I would have loved to duck behind my grocery cart or hide under the counter at the hospital and jump out and scream, "Run for your lives, the demons are everywhere!" I chuckle to even imagine people's reaction. But instead, I just listened to the gossip, which became more absurd each week; I let people think what they wanted. I didn't have time to care. I could have posted bizarre happenings and thoughts on Facebook, but I didn't. In fact, some people who read my posts never even heard the story. If I referred to our situation, it was vague. Well, it's unfortunate that people thrive off negativity and enjoy the misery of others.

My mind refocused on what I needed to accomplish that Saturday morning. I had been sitting on the back deck as the warm morning sun enveloped my tired bones. Sometimes, I just needed sunshine to feel human, if just for a few precious minutes. It was in those quiet moments that I could focus on me, the physical me that everyone else saw. My goodness, I thought, look at my skeletal body! I doubt buzzards would even circle my corpse. I was ashamed at my deathly ill appearance. I didn't even care to glimpse my reflection.

For some reason, I felt compelled to pray. I couldn't believe it. I approached God tentatively, like a scolded dog, sneaking back in to sit next to his master. God? I'm sorry. I haven't been making wise decisions. I need direction. I need to be grounded. Please God, I need Your help here; I'm making a big mess. Amen.

I leaned back on the lounge chair and closed my eyes. The sunshine and the prayer felt good; it felt right. I had been going through the motions of prayer. Suddenly, Seleria Jones' name came to my mind. I knew nothing of this woman, other than she operated her own daycare and was studying to be an evangelist. I reached down and picked up my phone. I put it back down. What would she think if I told her this unbelievable story? Would she even talk to me about it, or would she just brush the crazy white girl off? I found myself dialing her number, even though I had no idea what I was going to say as I listened to the rhythmic ringing. Hello? .....hello? My paralyzed vocal cords loosened enough to talk. I briefly told her the story, and she told me that she would call me right back. I thought she would never call, but she did. She was so encouraging and full of wisdom. Every word that came out of her mouth was positive. I felt a connection that I could not simply explain, but it was a connection I needed to feel.

Chapter 19

MY BODY, OR WHAT REMAINED OF IT, beckoned me towards death. It had given me plenty of warning signs aside from the desperate skeletal, gaunt, stooped reflection that I didn't even recognize anymore. My heartbeat was irregular; my crooked back was a knotted ball of agony and my appetite ceased to exist. I was a zombie. In fact, I felt dead already.

Not only was Joanie continuing to act out, now my oldest child, Janie, who was nine at the time, began to change, too. She started having fits of rage, and she cursed me with the same words that Joanie used in addition to hurtful words that were meant to manipulate my emotions. She was talking back when corrected, and if everything didn't go her way, she would rant, rage, and curse. She would say she hated her f-ing family and would call me an f- ing bitch. This was very out of character for her. Actually, that is language we don't use. This child, my firstborn, was deeply attached to me, more so than her younger sisters. She would tell me she loved me repeatedly, and when I left home for any reason, she always peeked through the blinds until my tail lights disappeared. She not only loved me, she deeply loved me. I knew she was being influenced to say those things. I just never thought or fathomed anything had been affecting her to this degree, but I had thus far only focused on the baby. Now it was clear that Satan did not care who he used to carry out his assault plans; he even used innocent children. He was using my children against me because he knew I'd give up my last breath to protect my girls. Just observing what was taking place, it seemed as if this particular entity was passing in and out of two of my children. My middle daughter, Jackie, was different. She accepted Jesus as her Savior at age four. Now many will argue that this is too young to fully comprehend, but this child had a deeper understanding of faith than many adults. She made a little book with her perception of the Bible, and on one page she wrote, God loves us, but stuff happens. At the bottom of the page she drew a tombstone with a flower beside it. I was impressed by her knowledge that life isn't a fairy tale. But she was adamant she needed to be baptized, or as she referred to it, "getting dunked." Although, she never exhibited any behavioral changes that were a cause for concern, she wasn't exempt from the evil. I have several pictures of her with a demonic face immediately behind her, above her and with its arms around her neck or shoulders. Given that knowledge, I felt like she had an external influence. And for whatever reason, she could see the spirits as clearly as Joanie, as she described their appearance with great detail, but she rarely discussed what she was seeing unless she felt comfortable that the person asking believed what she was saying. It really bothered her to hear people saying that I, or we, were crazy. She knew better, but didn't want to be labeled. She even drew a picture of the mean man coming into the bedroom with her and Joanie at night. She said the mean man was the short one that was greenish, with the flat head, funny ear/horn things with no hair, webbed fingers, and hooved feet. Personally, I think the title mean man could have applied to all of the intruders.

Chapter 20

AS WE SAT DOWN TO EAT ONE SATURDAY EVENING, Janie was whining excessively and refused to eat. She encircled her nose with her fist and whined and yelled so loudly with the complaint that her nose was burning, that it was disrupting the entire meal. I got up and motioned for her to get up and come with me, but she refused. I went to her and grabbed her arm firmly and told her to come outside and get some fresh air. Reluctantly, she went outside with me and stood on the patio. "Why are you acting like this, Janie? " "F*** you!" was the reply.

I looked down at her and noticed first her strained facial expression. Then I looked into eyes glazed with fierce hatred and anger. Now I'm not sure what prompted my response, but I leaned down until we were face to face and sternly said, "GET BEHIND ME SATAN!"

Janie let out a guttural growl and with clenched teeth, charged me, causing me to stumble backward. She said, "F*** you, bitch!" But it was not Janie's voice at all.

Thankfully, Jamie heard the commotion and came outside to ask what was going on, but it was self-explanatory in an instant, when the demon spoke through my child. I ran inside to call my mother-in-law to come get the other children. I instinctively knew this was very, very bad. As I ushered the younger two away from their meal and into the living room, I answered sternly to their why and what's wrong questions, to just do it! As I turned, Jamie was walking in with Janie over his shoulder, barely holding her legs as she writhed violently upside down. She was foaming at the mouth so profusely that it was dropping all over the floor. I pointed and said to take her to our room. I followed. She leaped out of his arms, landing with the grace of a cat and proceeded to tear our bed covers into a tangle. This voice coming from her was enraged, volatile, and pure evil. Her eyes were ....different, defiant, challenging. I noticed that her or its voice would rise in pitch and enunciate the last word in each sentence loudly. I had jokingly made the remark before my demon infestation, that my children needed an exorcism. I never dreamed one of them really would need one. I wished the yellow pages had a category for qualified exorcists. I left the room to call pastors, prayer warriors, and any person I thought would sincerely pray and not just gossip. Of course, my main prayer warrior was Mr. Charlie; I KNEW he would pray, and it wouldn't just hit the ceiling and bounce off. I felt the same about Loralyn and Seleria; they took prayer seriously.

I walked back to the bedroom to reassess the situation when I noticed Jamie was holding his pistol.

"What in the world are you doing with that? You can't shoot the demon, my God, put that up!"

Jamie was being cocky and commanding toward the spirit, but he did put the gun back in the closet.

Loralyn's parents came, as well as two of my cousins. Once I got off my cell, I placed it on the dresser and turned the audio on to record. By this time, she was somewhat more subdued. Somewhat. 'You FOOLS! This is my house now; this is my earth! I'll leave no one alive here, not even God! I will never leave; this is my body now!' Those were some of the statements that came from my nine-year-old while I was recording. One pastor, Bro. Leon Hickman, asked me to put him on the speaker phone so he could interact with this demonic presence, but that was unsuccessful; it wouldn't respond to the voice on the phone. Bro. Leon suggested we give Janie a break; so, we all left her standing on the bed, staring into a realm of existence that few care to acknowledge. I sat with my sister-in-law one night, allowing her to listen to the latest hellacious drama that we had to deal with in our home. She was in a state of disbelief at Janie's words and actions.

Even the fact that she was able to flip over a chest of drawers full of clothes was hard to believe, given her petite size. But the astounding thing that left us staring at one another with our chins on the floor, was what we heard on the audio clip, as it sat recording the silence in the bedroom where Janie, my child, buried behind evil, was alone, yet not alone.

A raspy, whispery male voice called her name, "Janie!" Then silence for a few seconds, as we leaned in closer to the cell, bumping heads, to make sure we were hearing what we thought we heard.

That same voice again, "Hey! You're stronger than even God now!"

Then, rapid footsteps approaching and the cell phone was bumped, picked up and set down, then footsteps retreating. This was a never ending horror story!

Chapter 21

JANIE SLOWLY BECAME MY LITTLE GIRL AGAIN, but I was still confused and very concerned because this entity wasn't cast out; it just retreated. She was in a daze, wandering around wide-eyed and quiet, wondering why people were at our house. I was standing in the kitchen still wringing my hands with worry, when I heard a commotion at the back door, which was open. A face appeared through the screen door, but it wasn't a demon; it was Julie, a high school friend and classmate. She and her boyfriend knew what was going on because her sister Rebecca, a nurse and co-worker, was one of the people I had called. Rebecca was a good friend. She is one of the slim few who dared to enter my home. She drove up one day with a couple of Christian books and religious artifacts. She acted like she was coming inside; so, I told her she didn't have to, that I'd come out.

She waved her hand at me and said, "Girl, I ain't worried."

That meant so much to me, though I did fear some of my boogers might follow her. Plus, she was going through her own hell, as her mother had just recently died unexpectedly, and it was devastating to their family. That was a true friend. Her sister, Julie, was loyal too.

Julie had been drinking, but said, "I know I ought not to come up here half lit, but Joy's my friend, and I'm gonna be here for her."

I thanked her and hugged her, and when we walked into the kitchen, Julie's wet boots slipped and down she went. She laughed at herself and to my surprise I heard a little giggle that I hadn't heard in quite a while; it was Janie.

Julie got up and hugged her and said, "How you doin', girl? Them ole demons messin' with you?" Janie nodded yes. Julie asked her if she could see them. She nodded yes.

"Can you see any now?" Janie nodded yes again. "Well, you just point 'em out to me, and I'll kick their a**! How does that sound?" Janie nodded yes and took Julie by the hand and led her around the house and pointed at a few places. I followed behind them, amused and amazed that Janie was responding so well. Julie surprised me as she did karate kicks at something only Janie and I saw; she was kicking as high as a horse in a bed of snakes. Janie loved it! Then she pointed to the ceiling in the corner.

"Whew! Girl, I'm too old to kick that one; so, I'll just have to tell that one to leave."

The one in the corner was purely demonic, but I think Julie would have faced it anyway. She walked right under the sneering face that had red eyes and two rows of about three inch horns above them.

She yelled, "Why don't you leave my friends alone, you son of a b***h! Just get the hell outta here and leave them alone!" I knew I would never forget how much therapy that was for Janie.

One of the ministers that I had spoken with during the previous night's events wanted us to be at New Zion UPC for the Sunday morning service. We were tired, but we went. He announced there would be a special prayer service for our family that evening. So again, we traveled back in hopes of freeing Janie. As we sat in the pew, Bro. Leon and the deacons were at the altar praying aloud before the service. I was so tired that I was numb. The remainder of this account was told to me by my husband, Bro Hickman, and his daughter, Sondra, who were all witnesses to round three demon evictions. Jamie said that during the prayer, he could hear growling and realized it was coming from me, but I was just sitting there. Bro Leon called us up front, and he approached Janie first and asked her how she felt. She shrugged and said okay. Before I realized what was happening, hands were placed upon my back, shoulders, and head, and prayers began. I felt like I was on a roller coaster going backwards, and I didn't like not being able to see where I was going. My voice changed into an angry male; Bro. Leon leaned forward to where I was kneeling and looked at me, face to face. He firmly and with the authority of Jesus, ordered the spirit to leave my body. The spirit sneered arrogantly and told him that I belonged to him; I had no choice.

Bro. Leon shook his no and laughed confidently, once again in its face, and said, "You can't have her; she's a child of God, bought by the blood of Jesus!"

The spirit, the same spirit that surfaced in my house earlier that year, apparently never left. This feverish prayer session extended way past regular church hours. The demon, the apparent ring leader, finally left. I became aware of my surroundings, everyone was sweating and breathing heavily, but everyone was smiling and rejoicing. My kids were playing in the sanctuary. Jamie and I experienced what it meant to be filled with the Holy Ghost and were baptized soon thereafter. I felt empowered, but my feet would soon lose grip of the road, again.

Chapter 22

I FELT EMPOWERED, BUT I LOST GROUND FAST. I would fall into every trap and get entangled in every snare that the enemy had in place. I was just predictable and pathetic. I was still able to audibly hear the entities speak, and I hated it with fierce resentment. I really just longed for my former, boring yet respectable life. The living room campground was up and running and I was on guard duty. This particular entity that loved using the f-word was my bitter enemy. He played games with my mind. He would gently pull the cover off of one of the girls, call them by name, and say, "Wake up! Wake up and f*** me!"

I would jump up and start praying or rebuking the demon and scoop up whichever child it was harassing. This was my nightly routine. Sometimes, it would just stomp and growl or stomp and hiss. Whatever scare tactic it used, it evoked fear in my children, fear that caused it to gain strength. I recall one particular day, the entity came spinning through as a "black tornado" as my child called it. It actually made the vertical blinds and curtain sway as it moved through the dining room. I had been sweeping that morning, and had a little pile of sand and trash swept up by the refrigerator. By the time it passed by where I was standing, it scattered my neat little pile of trash. I couldn't believe how it affected the tangible world surrounding it. It was changing me too, but I barely noticed. I was easily angered and would slam doors, kick furniture and would curse. Yes, even I began to curse. If I even thought about praying, I would be unable to breath, or get extremely nauseated. I still managed to utter short pleas and praises to God. I knew deep down He heard me, I just assumed I didn't deserve mercy. One evening, while the kids were all at my mother-in-law's, I was talking with Loralyn, sharing the latest events, and she wanted to pray before we hung up. I paused, but agreed. Fear gripped me because I knew I would be punished for consenting to divine intercession. I had been walking throughout the house while chatting with her and happened to be in the doorway of Janie's room when she started to pray, so I knelt there. Immediately, an invisible weight on my shoulders and back pushed me down onto my chest and then my entire body was compressed face down onto the carpet. I could hear Loralyn's voice boldly asking the Lord to deliver my family from the grips of evil. Amen.

"Joy? Joy? Are you okay?"

Silence. I stayed in that position for nearly thirty minutes. Having heard me describe in the past how I would be forced forward and held down, Loralyn knew what was occurring. She told me that she could hear me breathing, so she continued on with a one-sided conversation. She remained focused and positive and reassured me of God's protection. I finally heard the back door open and shut. Jamie was home bumping around in the kitchen, not knowing the predicament in the back room. Finally, he sauntered through the hallway and caught a glimpse of something on the floor; me. He asked me what in the world I was doing, as he heard Loralyn calling his name from the handset. She told him what happened. They exchanged worried words of concern for my safety. Jamie grabbed my arms and tried to lift me up, but I didn't budge. He described it much like having something really heavy anchoring me down, pulling me down as firmly as possible. He realized that prayer would help, so he placed a hand on my back, prayed, and then lifted me effortlessly. Jamie's prayers were effective, but we never prayed as a couple, even when told that we should.

Chapter 23

I DENIED MY OWN BASIC NEEDS, I believe, because I put my children's needs ahead of my own and because, deep down, I was punishing myself. When I did catch a nap, it was in the wee morning hours in my tub. I would soak in hot water and scroll through pictures I had taken the previous night. I woke up, I know, three different times and discovered my phone submersed in water. One would think I would have learned my lesson after the first time, but evidently, I'm a slow learner. I was obsessed with exposing my enemy, to prove that evil existed.

One particular morning, I realized that I had crossed a line—a dangerous line of obsession. When I was videoing the black fog in my bedroom, the demon said, "Hey, you looking for me?"

I couldn't believe it had the audacity to say that; so, as I sat in the tub at 4:30 in the morning, trying to get that video to upload on my phone, I was getting angry, frustrated, and beyond tired. I couldn't recall the last time I had slept over three or four hours. Most of that was in the tub; it was no wonder that my back hurt. Sometimes, the water was icy when I would wake up, and I was so stiff that I could barely move. I would literally crawl out of the tub and curl up on the rug and keep snoozing. As I futilely attempted to get the darn video to work, a song came on instead. I tried to turn it off. I was annoyed. Where did this song come from? I had never heard it, but it had a soothing tune so I sat and listened to the words. It was a song by Laura Story called "Blessings". Every verse was applicable to me, and I absorbed what God was trying to tell me. I replayed the song and smiled to myself. I couldn't delete it earlier, but it would play. God, you sure know how to handle me. And as the melody and words drifted around my entire being, the dam broke, and the floodgates opened. I cried the kind of cry that causes your stomach to hurt and for your sinuses to be clogged for a month. This got my attention. I was being blessed whether I knew it or not. The words replayed in my mind all afternoon:

> We pray for blessings, we pray for peace
> Comfort for family, protection while we sleep
> We pray for healing, for prosperity
> We pray for Your mighty hand to ease our suffering
> And all the while, You hear each spoken need
> Yet love us way too much to give us lesser things
>
> 'Cause what if Your blessings come through raindrops
> What if Your healing comes through tears
> What if a thousand sleepless nights are what it takes to know You're near
> What if trials of this life are Your mercies in disguise?
>
> We pray for wisdom, Your voice to hear
> And we cry in anger when we cannot feel you near
> We doubt your goodness, we doubt your love
> As if every promise from Your Word is not enough
> And all the while, You hear each desperate plea
> And long that we'd have faith to believe
>
> 'Cause what if Your blessings come through raindrops
> What if Your healing comes through tears
> What if a thousand sleepless nights are what it takes to know You're near
> What if trials of this life are Your mercies in disguise?

When friends betray us
When darkness seems to win, we know
That pain reminds this heart,
That this is not, this is not our home
It's not our home.

What if my greatest disappointments,
Or the aching of this life,
Is the revealing of a greater thirst this world can't satisfy?
What if trials of this life,
The rain, the storms, the hardest nights Are your mercies in disguise?
(Copyright April 2011 by Laura Story,
Columbia/INO Records/Sony Music Entertainment)

Chapter 24

I WOULD GET SO ANGRY WHEN JAMIE WAS HOME on the weekends; he would sleep like a baby even when the chaos was at its peak. He would tell me that God would protect the girls, but I felt that was my duty, to be there to hold and comfort them when they were scared. Jamie knew it was real, but he grew tired because it went on and on. He even wondered if I wanted it to stay, even though my physical appearance said otherwise. He was aggravated that I wouldn't take his advice, and I was angry because he didn't understand. When he was away at work during the week, we rarely even talked, and when we did, I tried not to mention the turbulent subject. I never even slept in the bed with him; if I did lie down, it was in one of the kids' rooms. One night I collapsed on top of the covers in Joanie's bed and allowed myself to drift off to sleep. I felt a hand grasp my left ankle. I looked up and saw nothing. I put my head back down, thinking I had been dreaming. I felt a quick jerk of my left leg and found myself jerked to the foot of the bed. The unseen hand continued to grip my leg and was slowly pulling me into the air. I was trying to grip the blanket, but it was pulled with me. I screamed for Jamie, like a child screams frantically for their mommy if they get scared. When Jamie came to the doorway, it let go of my leg, and I was left breathless on the bed. I told Jamie what just happened. He was annoyed that I was frightened. He scolded me like a child and told me I ought to be in there with him anyway. As he stomped back to the bed, I stomped back to the living room and thought to myself, if I was in there with him, it would probably chew me up and spit me out without waking Jamie. I chuckled under my breath because I could picture that scene.

The girls would play outside, and the mean man followed Joanie. Others were looking out the window. We drove two hours away to the water park, and it followed her. Janie stated that the bearded man followed her to school and would distract her by calling her name. Jackie added that she saw his face appear in the bathroom stall at school as well. At night, if we were in the car, the girls said different faces would appear in the windows. This was common. When we would arrive back home, the girls would refuse to get out of the car because they felt surrounded. It just infuriated me that not only were we prisoners in our home but we were also prisoners in our lives. The song, "Set Me Free" by Casting Crowns started playing in my mind.

I knew people thought I was hallucinating. I knew people thought I had a breakdown. I knew they thought I must surely need some kind of medication. I knew if I had been on the outside looking in, I would have been skeptical. Somebody who thought I was not capable of caring for my children reported me to the child protective services. I realize they were endangered each time I drove them anywhere in my sleep-deprived state, but I didn't think that way at the time. I was just into survival mode, closing out the world and hunkering down over my children to survive. I was determined to survive, and I had been refreshed enough spiritually by now that I realized this horrendous ordeal was changing me into the mother, wife, neighbor, friend, and Christian that I was supposed to be all along. I saw everything and everybody in a new light. And I had the wisdom and discernment to know who would try to influence me in a negative manner, and I limited contact with those people. Even organized religion was viewed in a different manner. My eyes were opened, and my faith moved to a new level.

Chapter 25

ONE DAY AROUND LUNCH, I was chasing Joanie around when I noticed a sedan and a police car drive up. I knew immediately who they were, and I knew why they were here. I took in a deep breath, opened the door, and welcomed them into my home. The lady told me I had been reported to OCS, but she couldn't disclose by whom, but I already had a strong suspicion. It didn't matter now; I had been dealt another hand, and it was time to put on my poker face and play cards. This was an annoying distraction that I had to face and overcome. God, please help me again, I said sincerely to myself. The case worker could look at me physically and surmise that I was going through something, and she could see the desperation in my tired eyes. She listened to what I had to say, and of course, she couldn't say either way her opinion, but I knew she was open-minded from the look in her eyes. She also came back and met with Jamie. She advised the best way to clear myself would be to pass a psychiatric evaluation and the quickest way to do that would be to sign myself into a facility for 24 hours. She found a place in New Orleans, and said I needed to be there first thing the next day. Jamie was going back to work, so, my friend Rebecca agreed to take me after we dropped off our kids at school. I hugged my girls tightly that morning. I just kept telling myself that I had to be strong for them. I thought I would see them the next day. Rebecca and I joked some, talked serious some, and sometimes rode in silence with our own thoughts. I felt like an abandoned pet as I watched my friend leave me and I heard the lock click as the door closed to the insane world outside. I put aside all preconceived notions regarding the mental health system that I had formed as a nurse. I walked in with an open mind. I was taken in a room with a female employee where I had to turn in my belt, shoe laces, makeup, cell phone, and anything that could harm me or others. Then she asked me to drop my pants and shake my panties. I looked at her with all the seriousness I could muster and I said that I don't usually do that unless I get to know them better. She never cracked a smile. She just motioned for me to pull my pants down.

I sat before the psychiatrist with my jeans being held up with two Velcro straps. I recounted the events that led to my being in his office. His face twisted in confusion.

"So who told you to come here?"I replied with, "Child protective services. They told me I needed an evaluation and this was the best way to expedite the process."

He laughed. "Well, it's a good thing that everyone in society who has encounters with the supernatural isn't admitted for an evaluation, or the entire system would need to be revamped."I replied, "That's crazy."

"Exactly," he said as he pointed at me with his pen .He never prescribed any medications, thankfully. I had worried they would attempt to give me something, and I wanted to fully cooperate or that may look bad on my part. I went through a battery of psychological testing and was even assessed by a medical physician to rule out medication side effects, brain tumor, or electrolyte imbalance. I was cleared but ended up staying six nights to complete everything and get through the red tape. Bro. Leon was faithful to call. One of the ER physicians from the hospital where I used to work came to see me and brought me a much needed jacket. And faithful Rebecca and Julie drove to the city to visit. All of them were so supportive. That really helped.

I can honestly say that God got me through that valley. I remember feeling out of place. I was so reserved and had never been outgoing socially. In times past, in these situations, I would have isolated myself and become introverted in order to cope. But I found myself mingling among the other patients, getting to know them. My first night there, I was freezing cold. I felt like I was sleeping on a board, but I was not accustomed to even sleeping in a bed period, so, I dared not complain. The security guard came through routinely and shined his flashlight in everyone's bed. I asked him if I could get some water because my throat was sore.

He sharply replied, "Get it from the faucet!" I suddenly wasn't as thirsty anymore. The next morning my throat was really sore, and the coffee smelled divine even though I rarely drank it. I strolled out of my room, following my nose. "Get back in the room NOW! It's not time for coffee!" I realized he was speaking to me. I timidly asked what time was coffee. "5:30!"

I looked down at my watch. It was 5:28. So, I strolled to my room, turned around, and strolled out to get my coffee. I went out to sit in the smoking area to try to thaw out. It was September, but in the Big Easy, it was tolerable and mild. A tall, lanky black man who appeared to be in his late fifties joined me. He was rummaging through the ashtray, looking for salvageable remains that he could get a drag or two from. He was friendly, talkative, and knew how to play the system. As I sized him up, I noticed he had on six layers of shirts underneath his jacket. The top layer was soiled with stains, food particles, and had little burn holes where it was exposed. I sat for a split second, my mind focused on surviving the hypothermic environment, and decided I was going to have to be clever and play the game, too. I tried my best to be cool.

I said, "Hey bro, I'll give you three dollars for that gray sweatshirt."

It was three layers down, so I was hoping it was clean. He whipped it off really quickly and gave it to me before I had a chance to change my mind. It wasn't the cleanest, but it was warm. I smiled to myself as he sat peeling the dead skin off of his feet, roll it up and attempt to light it and smoke it as if it were a joint.

All of the counselors, physicians, and social workers believed me, except for one. His mind was closed before my mouth opened to speak. He reminded me of Liam Neeson. He seemed perturbed that the psychiatrist did not suggest medication to control my "delusions." He tried his best to break me, psychologically speaking. My oldest and youngest daughters both had a birthday that week. I told him, the day my baby turned three, that I had completed all the tests that were required and I wanted to go home because I didn't want to miss it.

He looked me square in the eyes and said, "Aww...doesn't that suck?"

I felt like ripping his ears off, but instead, I smiled and replied, "Yes, it sure does."

I read my Bible a lot. I stayed outside with the smokers. They were the sanest people there. I grew to love our little clique. Although, it felt like a safe haven, there was three occasions that a violent young man would escape the guard and come to the patio area, slinging metal chairs and fighting. That was the only times I felt frightened while there. This admission changed how I feel about mental illness. What was funny, was that amidst the whirlwind of their own nightmares, the other patients knew that I stuck out like a sore thumb. I recall them cheering loudly as I rolled my suitcase through the exit. That had been a hard experience, but I got a little rest. Gnarls Barkley's, "Crazy" kept playing in my mind as my brother-in-law drove me back to civilization. I smiled. I was happy to get that trial over with. I posted this statement on Facebook in order for the person that was probably still gloating from my experience, to let them and others know that I was getting back on my feet:

I COULD BE ANGRY OR JUST PLAIN BITTER. SIX NIGHTS SPENT IN AN ADULT PSYCHIATRIC FACILITY. ABSENT FROM TWO DAUGHTERS' BIRTHDAY PARTIES. STRIPPED OF ALL DIGNITY, PRIDE AND RIGHTS. SUBJECTED TO VIOLENCE FROM OTHER PATIENTS AND REPEATED ATTEMPTS BY STAFF TO BREAK MY PSYCHOLOG- ICAL MAKEUP AND EMOTIONAL BACKBONE. EVEN AFTER BEING DEEMED COMPE- TENT AND FAR FROM DELUSIONAL, DURING THE FIRST TWENTY FOUR HOURS, BY A PSYCHIATRIST. NOT, I REPEAT, NOT DELUSIONAL! NOR SCHIZOPHRENIC, BIPOLAR NOR DEPRESSED. CLEARED MEDICALLY BY A GENERAL MEDICINE PHYSICIAN. NO CHEMICAL IMBALANCE, NO BRAIN TUMOR AND NO SIDE EFFECTS OF PARKINSON'S MEDICATIONS. PASSED INTENSE PSYCHOLOGICAL TESTING, WRITTEN AND ORAL. SCRUTINIZED AT EVERY ANGLE. AND NOTHING. NOTHING, THAT IS, BUT A CLEAN BILL OF MENTAL HEALTH. NO MIND-ALTERING MEDICINE PRESCRIBED OR GIVEN.

SO, WHY AM I NOT ANGRY OR BITTER? I MADE THE MOST OF A BAD SITUATION. I LOOKED AT THE GOOD, INSTEAD OF THE BAD. I LAUGHED, WHEN I COULD HAVE CRIED. I HELD FIRM TO GOD, INSTEAD OF DWELLING ON THE SCHEMES OF THE DEVIL (AND THAT INCLUDES THE PEOPLE WHO DON'T BELIEVE IN HIS EXISTENCE,

YET CARRY OUT HIS WORK). I WAS LITERALLY HUMBLED DURING THIS EYE-OPENING EXPERIENCE. I MET THE MOST AMAZING GROUP OF PEOPLE (YES, THE OTHER PSYCH PATIENTS, WHO ARE TREMENDOUS ASSETS TO OUR SOCIETY) AND FORMED SEVERAL CLOSE FRIENDSHIPS. I LEARNED THAT YOU CAN'T JUDGE A BOOK BY ITS COVER OR LACK OF ONE.

I AM NOT ANGRY OR BITTER TOWARDTHE WELL-MEANING PERSON WHO CALLED THE CHILD PROTECTIVE SERVICES, THINKING I WAS SURELY PSYCHOTIC OR DELU-SIONAL AND ENDANGERING MY CHILDREN. WHAT I WAS, HOWEVER, WAS TIRED. TIRED FROM LACK OF SLEEP AND SACRIFICING MY OWN PHYSICAL HEALTH TO PRO-VIDE COMFORT AND SECURITY TO MY CHILDREN. IF ONE DOES NOT UNDERSTAND WHAT IS OCCURRING IN MY HOME, THEN DO NOT PASS JUDGEMENT BEFORE GOING TO THE SOURCE. IT IS WHAT IT IS. AND IT IS SOMETHING MEDICATION AND PSY-CHIATRISTS CANNOT FIX . . . ONLY GOD.

Chapter 26

THE DEVIL WOULD NEED NEW TRICKS to continue his war on my faith. I bragged too soon; I fell right back into staying up all night again. I was determined to sleep by trying sleeping pills, but I didn't like the way they made me feel the next day. I then got the idea that a glass of wine might help. It did relax me, and I slept. Then I started buying and drinking more, getting a variety because I knew nothing about alcohol. I was sitting in my bed, relaxed with my Long Island Iced Tea watching television. One thing I noticed -- once I drank enough, I didn't guard the girls; I'd literally pass out sometimes. Late night television was awful; there was nothing to watch. I flipped through and saw a naked love scene. I continued watching. I was intrigued. That became my nightly routine and if Jamie was home, I would drink and watch television in one of the kids' rooms. One night, I realized I was on the phone ordering porn from the television company. My God, I thought, I've never wanted alcohol, and I've always abhorred pornography. It was disgusting, nauseating; yet, there I sat and didn't know why. I felt as if someone else was looking through my eyes. I got up one night, staggered to the bathroom and fell down. I crawled to my bathtub to pull myself up and happened to see someone in the mirror, someone on the verge of death, someone barely holding on to reality. I staggered backwards and leaned my back on the wall. The song "Voodoo" by Godsmack began pounding inside my head. "I'm not the one that's so far away, when I feel the snake bite into my veins, never did I wanna be here again, and I don't remember why I came."

I slid down the wall and sat on the floor with my skeletal arms around my bent legs. I wanted to cry, but I couldn't. "Candles raise my desire, why I'm so far away, No more meaning to my life, No more reason to stay, Freezing feeling, Breathe in, Breathe in, I'm coming back again."

I raised my head and looked around the dim bathroom; faces materialized from the dark shadows, and I just stared as my internal radio kept blaring. "Hazing clouds rain on my head, Empty thoughts fill my ears, Find my shade by the moon light, Why my thoughts aren't so clear, Demons dreaming, Breathe in, Breath in, I'm coming back again..."

When I woke up with a fierce headache, daylight was streaming inside the room. I got up and started another day after saying a short prayer. "God I'm awfully close to the edge, please help me back to the life You want me to live. Amen and thank you."

My cousin Donna started helping me clean the house. She was leery because she knew that the supernatural was real. She knew somebody who knew somebody who could help. Here we go again; this is getting old. Nobody can get rid of this thing. Two ladies came one Saturday afternoon. I didn't even follow them inside to see what they were going to do. It didn't matter. The ladies came staggering outside; they looked tired, drained. They both stated there were multiple spirits in our home. They said one was the boss, or in charge, and he was keeping the other entities. Well, we had heard that before. The husband of the younger lady appeared to be a Native American. He walked around the house, inside and out. He said our home was on a ley line. What the heck is a ley line? I wanted to know; so, we could get rid of it. He explained that ley lines were geographical alignments in the earth that were pathways of energy that spirits travel on in order to obtain energy. This supposedly ran right through our home. They said they would return and bury crystals along the line and that would help quiet the activity. They told us of portals in our home that needed to be moved. The older woman said she got the mean man to leave. I was skeptical. She said that she asked him nicely. You have to give them respect, she said. She wanted me to give something that had terrorized my family for nearly two years respect? That,

I could not—and would not—do. I was doubtful of her.

Things were calmer, and I didn't think I had seen Joanie whispering to herself lately. But Janie was still very volatile. I had not been myself for a month. I was still drinking at night and watching adult movies, but no one knew this. This dark side that emerged hid well within the real Joy. By day, I could smile and go through the motions. Seleria was telling me scriptures to read, but I never did. We began going to Mt .Hermon UPC again with Bro Garcia and I enjoyed it, but the heavy feeling in my chest was smothering. I would get dazed and sleepy and I would lean to the right, nearly onto the person sitting next to me. My language became less than lady-like. I recall my Jackie reprimanding me one day, saying that I was not supposed to talk like that and asked why I was even doing that, because I had never talked like that before. I sarcastically told her that her sister's must be rubbing off. More and more frequently, the spirits within our home would go through me, and at night, they would hover all over me. They were attracted to all of us. It was unsettling for me, so I know it was scary for the kids. Many times, Joanie acted as if she was afraid to look at me, but I knew why she was scared. The spirits would get in front of my face and she could not see her mother. I knew this for certain because I had taken pictures of myself when I felt "something" around my head and I had four pictures that were clearly not me, yet they were. These pictures were disturbing. Little Joanie figured out on her own that if she wore sunglasses at night, she would not see the dark shadows. My child slept in sunglasses; that broke my heart. I recall fearing the boogeyman as a child, but I can't imagine actually seeing him and hearing him talk. My prayer warrior, Mr. Charlie, was getting frail as he battled cancer. This Christian man, though suffering his own hell, continued to call to check on us. Many times, as with everyone else, I would say we were fine. I didn't want to burden him. Yet, I think he could tell I was not fine simply by the sound of my voice. Seleria continued to encourage and pray as well as my best friend Loralyn. The prayers of others sustained me when my faith wavered.

Chapter 27

ONE NIGHT, AS I SCROLLED THROUGH FACEBOOK, I noticed a conversation between two guys regarding one of the paranormal activity movies. I made a comment that I had been there, done that and had the t-shirt. I expressed that I had NO desire to watch it because I was living it. It stirred Peter's curiosity. I briefly told him the situation, and he wanted to help. I hardly knew Peter. I didn't know how he could help, but he couldn't hurt. He was not an ordained minister, but was well versed in scripture. He knew his Bible. He asked a million questions and was an insightful and keen observer. Sometimes, he really annoyed me with questioning every time I would blink out of rhythm or would breathe crooked, but he was good with Janie.

His main focus was surrounding the event in Honduras. He said these things either had to be hanging on to objects from there, or there was unconfessed sin. I thought everything had been burned from that trip, but I recalled buying gifts for my parents and grandparents; Peter told me to get all of those items together. A prayer team was assembled for my house and remotely. Now part of me did not believe those souvenirs held any real significance, but as I left home to gather up the things, I felt that familiar drugged, lethargic state. I got everything together and headed home. I had to struggle to stay awake. That was scary. I had already wrecked both of our vehicles, falling asleep at the wheel. And I can't count the times God awakened me, seconds before a collision. I even fell asleep driving down our long driveway as I was trying to get to my mother n laws for Thanksgiving, a couple months earlier and Jamie finally came back home and found me and informed me that I had scorched the dumplings. I hated the way this thing made me slip into this catatonic state. As I drove slowly up to the garage, a large entity appeared on the back wall. I stopped the vehicle and turned off the key; the fog began to flow toward the hood. In the name of Jesus, I command you to stop! I command you! But it came rolling through the vents like billows of smoke and surrounded me. I had no authority through Christ at that time, I was knee-deep in sin. I couldn't speak or move; I was dazed, in a stupor. When I roused I realized that a little over an hour had passed. I had drool down my chin. Then I noticed something else; I had urinated on myself. Oh my goodness, I thought as I dialed Peter's number.

"Are you alright? I can barely hear you."

I was finally able to speak loud enough for him to understand, and I told him the disturbing events. A male voice interrupted our conversation, as it had done before, saying "f*** you" and "You are going to die!" Peter immediately rebuked the voice with scripture or he would burst forth singing a gospel song. Even when a pair of eyes materialized on the wall inside my home, Peter quoted scripture with authority as the eyes squinted down at him with hatred.

Saturday morning came with graying clouds forming. The prayer teams were assembled. I thought we were going to free Janie from her anger and rage. We sat outside under the garage as Peter walked outside to the little pile of Honduran relics, doused them with diesel, and set them on fire. I could not see the fire being set, but as soon as it was lit, I felt something on my back, right under my neck; it was a drilling sensation. Peter's dad was a minister and was sitting beside me. I looked up at him and told him to anoint my back, quick! I felt something was entering through my back. I lost consciousness. I ended up on the hard, cold cement as the rain began to fall. It took four men to restrain me, and I still ended up halfway in the rain. The ordeal lasted for two and a half hours. Cursing, spitting and a promise from the demon that he would return were, I was told, the events of the day. It ended finally when Peter grabbed my jaw, thrust it open, and poured blessed oil directly down my throat. My voice broke through, telling the spirit to get out. I asked the men to let me up on my knees. I began to pray, and immediately my mouth opened, and I was told I exhaled and exhaled longer than humanly possible. I was told my mouth appeared larger than it should. And everyone who was outside agreed the stench was horrendous. I collapsed onto the cement, face first, which left me with a nice shiner on one eye and cheek.. Jamie took me to our bedroom, and I slept for several hours. One of the local pastors pulled Jamie aside. He was only outside briefly to witness the events, but he told my husband that he didn't think that was real although he gave no definite reasoning other than he had never seen anything like that before. Well, most haven't, and upon further research into the matter, no two exorcisms are alike. It depends on the spirit within, the rank, the characteristics of the demon. This is not a textbook science; neither is religion. This pastor told Jamie he thought I had multiple personalities. Jamie was polite, but he was livid. When I awoke, he asked me what the symptoms of multiple personalities were. I told him, from what I recalled from nursing school, that the first main symptom was a period of amnesia. For example, someone would be gone for days in which they had no clue as to even who they were. Also, they experience depersonalization and derealization, which means they don't view themselves as real or the world around them.

He looked at me and said, "You won't believe it, but that's what the pastor diagnosed you with."

Well, I wonder how many cases of that has he seen; did he minor in psychology? And by the way, how many exorcisms has he witnessed? Plus, I had never had periods of amnesia or felt like I wasn't real and I knew without a doubt the events in our home were very real. I did later apologize to this pastor because I held bitterness in my heart towards him for not understanding.

I told Jamie, "Don't worry about it. People are just searching for scientific causes to reason with the supernatural realm which they don't understand." I would jokingly state that this was Joy #2 when my husband would call to check on us.

The very next day I noticed my spine, which had been curved, was straight. I couldn't believe my eyes. I went to see the orthopedic surgeon for confirmation. This miracle would be short lived. It wasn't long; the cycle resumed. Peter said that it was either an object I had overlooked or unconfessed sin. Seleria said that everyone in the family was not delivered yet. But I had done something stupid, two things actually. First, I did have an unconfessed sin besides the drinking and porn. During the time that was occurring, I began having sexual thoughts and fantasies. I was approached for sex and consented to the act. As soon as it started, I knew it was wrong; I did not enjoy it, and I felt disgusted with myself. What had I done? I just fell into another trap that would ruin my good girl reputation. How could I have done that with someone who I wasn't even attracted to at all? How could I be unfaithful to my husband, who I loved? How could I break the sacred vows I took before God? I tried desperately to hide this sin, but I was not very good at lying. I confessed to Jamie. This sin occurred during the alcohol/porn stage. The drinking and adult move viewing stopped with the last exorcism. I had not told anyone about that; that was not totally me. Did the devil "make" me commit adultery? No, but the circumstances surrounding the madness that was taking place in our home, not to mention my severe sleep deprivation, influenced me to make a very bad choice. However, I felt as if someone else were still looking through my eyes. That feeling occurred in church as well. I began having sexual thoughts again, I felt like I was being urged to seduce the preacher. I would not do that, I thought, and my will overrode the notion. Satan was trying to destroy everyone's reputation that was involved. But the second stupid thing besides the unconfessed sin was, I had confronted the spirit that was attacking Janie, and I know, without a doubt, it reentered my body. I learned that unless one is spiritually strong, she should never get in the boxing ring with the devil. I got my lights knocked out. I was cocky, arrogant after the exorcism, because I felt so free. Now here I was, bound ... again, but at least I knew it and desired it gone ... forever. I told the Bro Garcia of my suspicions of reentry. One night as we were singing at the end of the service, the pastor noticed that I was under spiritual attack, so he walked to the pew in front of me to anoint me with blessed oil. I was told I reached up and encircled his necktie with one hand and attempted to choke him. I ended up on the floor between the pews; so, they moved me to the altar. I was told I was growling and hissing. Donna, my cousin, was wondering how this could be real; she said, until I screamed in a deep, unrecognizable voice in the pastor's face, to "f*** you," then she knew beyond any doubt. And that's when she told her husband to leave because she knew spiritually he should not be present. After that night, I felt so good - relief, and much peace. I did, however, have one last showdown before admitting and begging God for His forgiveness and truly and with no doubts, knew I was delivered, redeemed and free.

I was soaking in a very hot tub of water one day around lunch to ease my back pain, when Seleria texted from the school where she was working just to check on me. She had become not only a friend and mentor, but a mother figure to me. A very masculine appearing spirit materialized inside the bathroom door so I text back that I couldn't talk that "it" was there. She replied to call if I wanted her to pray. As the demon drew closer, I ripped the little vial of blessed oil off of my necklace and threw it toward the shadow man and it landed and broke on the floor with no effect. My cell phone rang several times. Seleria texted to answer when she called. I was slipping out of consciousness, but texted NO, right before I dropped the cell on the floor beside the tub. Her texts that followed from her were prayers, pleading the blood of Jesus over me. To Seleria's utter shock, words started appearing on her phone that were not English and appearing so rapidly that she knew was not humanly impossible. She grabbed a Christian co-worker to pray silently as she earnestly prayed and text for this thing to flee. This intercessory prayer continued for nearly an hour. Finally, I awoke, drained and exhausted. I picked up my cell phone and stared in disbelief at a line of text messages that I could not read, but I realized it wasn't just random letters. I sat dazed as I dialed my voicemail and listened to the desperate, yet bold and confident words offered to God for my safety and release. I scanned the room to find I was alone and that thankfully my mind clear. I texted Seleria to let her know that I was okay. The text language was soon translated and was Portuguese. The words were directed at Seleria, even referring to her by her nickname. The words threatened that the new army of God would be destroyed and that I would die. Both of us were in total shock at this event, it felt like a dream, yet we both held reality in our hands. I knew I had to confess one last, ignorant, incomprehensible thing I had done that gave this particular entity a "legal right" to keep re-entering my physical body. First, I told Jamie. It was during one the darkest periods, when I was extremely sleep deprived, nearing physical death, and could audibly hear the demons speak. The mean man appeared to me one morning and made a proposition. He promised my children would be left alone, with no further torment and would have peace if I would allow it to enter my body at will to gain strength. I knew I didn't have much physical reserve left, but I was willing to die for my kids to have peace. I was willing to burn in Hell if need be, to offer my children life without fear. I agreed. My Lord, I just made a deal with the devil, I don't deserve forgiveness, I deserved death. The old crafty devil did not uphold his end of the deal. My girls continued to live in fear in our home. I was so ashamed of my stupidity, I had never asked God to forgive me. After the bathtub attack, I was ready, ready to break every chain of spiritual bondage. I was finally able kneel before God, beg His forgiveness, shed bitter tears of repentance, and literally felt arms hugging me as if I were the prodigal son. I now had the spiritual authority to break the pact I had made with the enemy. Through the authority of Christ, I ejected the final piece of trash that was poisoning my existence. This was "my demon" and I, backed with God's grace, made it leave. I would have done backflips if I were able, I was FREE! I recalled the time at Mt. Hermon UPC, after my deliverance session, a humble church member knelt by me and recited John 8:36 "If the Son therefore shall make you free, ye shall be free indeed." He repeated this several times and asked me to repeat it too. I didn't grasp the magnitude of that verse until the last chain fell from my wrist. I was free and I cried tears of joy and relief. I couldn't stop laughing and smiling and I knew God was nodding in approval and smiling too.

Chapter 28

MY OLDEST DAUGHTER CONTINUED TO STRUGGLE. One night she got out of the tub and came into the kitchen where I was rushing around to cook supper.

She raised her arm and said, "Mommy, look at this."

I glanced and told her it looked like a scratch. She asked then if I knew what it meant. I replied, "Yeah, it means you've got a scratch."

She was growing impatient. She then yelled, "I know that, but what does it mean?"

Annoyed, I stopped and looked and immediately realized it was a symbol. I asked her how it had gotten under her arm. She claimed she didn't know, but her voice and eyes told me she knew. Her sisters were in the room, but no one was giving straight answers. I took pics of the symbol and forwarded one to an acquaintance who was familiar with the occult. I was told that the symbol was a satanic cross with Satan's trident or pitchfork on top. My question was why and how? I was disturbed and felt uncertainty and fear creeping into my mind. After all, a similar thing had happened to Joanie in the tub with her cousin one night. They both erupted from the tub in an explosion of bubbles and water, screaming in terror. Joanie had a red, raised mark on her chest and neither child ever spoke a word as to what happened. I began calling pastors who were familiar with what we had been going through. People in general would like to think that sort of thing only happens in the movies, so I wasn't surprised at all by their responses that suggested perhaps she did that to herself or she was secretly involved in the occult, or she or I need further counseling.. That was the last time I would panic and be made to look like I was crazy. I finally could see the enemy's mode of operation. Make mom panic, then make her look crazy, ruin her reputation, ruin her witness. I prayed over the situation, gave my worries to God. Exactly what I should've been doing the entire time. But, Janie was becoming more volatile than ever. She attacked me physically from behind while driving. She punched me in the head and chest, and she attempted to jump out of our moving vehicle. That was not her first attempt. Counseling had not helped, either. I refused to let this destroy us. I had been visiting a nondenominational church in a nearby town. Prophet Love recognized what her problem was and placed his anointed hands on each side of Janie's head and prayed against the demonic spirit that was affecting her mind. He prayed fervently to cancel the assignment of this demonic spirit. God had intervened and Janie, to my amazement, started to be herself soon after. I was relieved to see her smile and laugh and to be relaxed. We sold our home and settled into a rental house temporarily. I was urged to have our now empty house of horror professionally investigated to add validity to our claims. I didn't really need validation myself because as we moved the last few pieces of furniture, light bulbs exploded in anger, making a big mess. PSP returned, not capturing much evidence, but Jereme returned the following night and documented more than enough proof that something remained. His desire to truly see people escape their living nightmare, prompted him to form his own professional team, called Ghost Quest. Society may refer to spirits as ghosts, I figure, because it sounds less threatening than the word demon. Nonetheless, upon moving, my health began to improve and Janie began to heal. I knew she was finally free from her private torture. She and I were riding down the road one day as she stared out the window. She mentioned what a beautiful day it was and I agreed. She then asked a question that I didn't grasp at first. She asked, "Mommy, how come I've never seen the sun before?" I was dumbfounded at the paradoxical question at first. Then I smiled with tears in my eyes and replied with a cracking voice, "Because we are finally out of the darkness."

I thought of my beloved Mr. Charlie, who had passed away before our trial ended. I would have been so ashamed had he been here to see how low I sank, but I could feel him smiling with happiness that good does overcome evil.

This two-year journey was unrelenting and treacherous. My relationship with God waxed and waned as my faith gasped for air to breathe. My life had become absent of light, I was spiritually blinded by lack of knowledge and I allowed the forces of darkness to conceal and obscure the truth. Ultimately, I was broken to the point of utter helplessness. I had no choice but to raise my arms to heaven and submit EVERY aspect of myself to Him. I had to learn after repeated failure that I was never in control. I was HIS, I was forgiven, redeemed and molded into the Christian He intended me to be. Never underestimate the power of evil or disbelieve that demons are in fact real beings, as the Bible states. Christians use their denial as an excuse to live in ignorant bliss. Though it seems rational not to believe in something unless everyone can see it, but the denial of things due to limited experience is absurd. Too many stumble over reality on occasion, but most get up and dust their knees off as if nothing happened. They look truth in the eye and deny it. But reality is that just because one refuses to believe in something, doesn't make it disappear. It's no wonder that truth is more powerful than fiction, fiction has to make sense. What occurred in our home did not make sense, it surpassed my understanding and caused me to question my own sanity at times, but I held on to a thread of faith and it turned into the rope that God used to pulled my family out of the darkness.

Out of the darkness
Back in his light
Free from the evil
That stole my nights
No more fear
The cross in my sight
I held it before me
As i stood up to fight
Cried out to god
He knew my plight
I begged for mercy
With all of my might
Mountain behind me
Gazed up at the height
Scaled it in his time
He held my hand tight
Raised up my sword
Evil took flight
His word in my heart
My strength ignites
Never go back
Wide path not right
Never ever doubt
Not even slight
Peace in my soul
My eyes again bright
Amazing grace
Back in his light.

CPSIA information can be obtained at www.ICGtesting.com
Printed in the USA
BVOW02s0601170316

440532BV00003B/168/P

9 780989 474818